SWEET REVENGE

SWITCH
PRESS

SWEET REVENGE is published by
Switch Press
a Capstone imprint
1710 Roe Crest Drive
North Mankato, Minnesota 56003   ("Land of 10,000 Lakes")   BAKES
www.mycapstone.com

tsk tsk

Cataloging-in-Publication Data is available on
the Library of Congress website.
ISBN: 978-1-63079-089-9 (paperback)
ISBN: 978-1-63079-090-5 (eBook)

Printed and bound in Canada.
010796S18

SWITCH
PRESS

Sweet REVENGE

PASSIVE-AGGRESSIVE DESSERTS
FOR YOUR EXES & ENEMIES

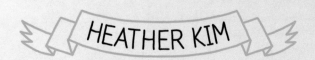

HEATHER KIM

Dedicated to the
EPICALLY BURNED

CONTENTS

REVENGE IS BEST SERVED *WARM*

Dumped by your oh-so significant other? BFF steal your one-and-only? Lab partner a more-than-periodic no-show?

Don't take these battles online, people. (Seriously, don't do that, ok?) Instead, take all that frustration, jealousy, and I-want-to-rip-your-heart-out-and-feed-it-to-my-freaking-Pekingese murderous anger into the kitchen.

Because despite what you've heard, revenge is best served warm.

That's right, all you Burned and Beaten Down, get out your heaviest rolling pins, sharpest cleavers, and most blistering torches, and kill your enemies & exes . . . with kindness. Or at least bake them some killer cakes.

And no, I'm not talking about baking a Mr. Yuk-face-approved, "Come on, have a bite, Snow White," poisonous apple pie. I'm talking about the real deal: 100% delicious AF cakes, cookies, and candies. (Oh my!) I'm talking about consciously choosing to be generous and to make fat, happy things, even for the worst of the worst.

Why? Because kindness is rare, folks. It's radical. Like baking, kindness takes time, energy, and effort, and those efforts are wholeheartedly returned. Trust me, they are. Somehow, they always are. For me, those returns have been absolute happiness, in all its dippy, dumb, lovely, joyful glory.

I hope the same for you.

So, come on. Stop your bitchin' and get in that kitchen. Bake that loser ex a half dozen D-Bagels or a pan of Go Fudge Yourself. Gift your former friend a You're the Devil Food Cake or a What a Piece of Sheet Cake. And give that waste of O_2 a scoop of When I Think of Us, Ice Cream. Let them taste your post-them happiness, and see what comes next . . .

Now that's some SWEET REVENGE.

Kindly,

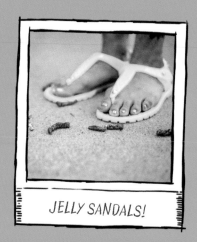

JELLY SANDALS!

GOOD LUCK!

EGG ROLL TAT :)

HOME

NEON FOOD

PUT A RING ON IT

GRAB LIFE BY THE MILK BALLS

AKA HOW TO USE THIS BOOK
AKA WTF IS SWEET REVENGE?

Fyi:

Before we go any further, full disclosure: this is a cookbook. Like, for real. For real-real even. Let's just get that straight from the get-go, ok?

This isn't, for example, some kind of *Dr. Love's Guide to Discovering Your Whole Delicious Self* (which you most certainly should). Nor is this the *Life-Changing Magic of Tidying Your Teenage Life* (#messy4lyfe) or the *Ultimate Path to Finding Your True Soul Mate* (unless your "true soul mate" just happens to be chocolate cake, then yeah, maybe . . .).

This book is not your therapist. Or your friend. Or even a *SHRIEK!* parent. This book should never — I mean, NEVER-EVER — be considered a substitute for IRL relationship advice and/or counseling.

Because, all together now: THIS. IS. A. COOKBOOK.

And that concludes today's public service announcement

That said, here's some advice: You can't hate-tweet your ex when you're knuckles-deep in molasses. (Okay sure, technically, you could. But your 140-character declaration of always-and-forever, one-and-only love will most certainly get you in an even stickier mess — and/or cost you a new iPhone.)

I mean, think about it, baking is the perfect outlet for all that pent-up, stood-up-in-a-McDonald's-parking-lot-on-prom-night-in-an-overpriced-backless-dress RAAAGGE.

Baking takes thought, exactitude, and above all else . . . patience. (Ever try waiting for lava cake to cool? That's a serious Jedi mind trick right there.)

Some people even call baking a science. But maybe we should think of it as taste-bud meditation, Pilates for your papillae, or — better yet — kitchen kickboxing! Where else can you BEAT, WHIP, POUND, and CREAM something without risking serious OITNB (but in a way-less-funny way) jail time?

FLAMIN' HOT BLISS

Seriously, if you consider yourself a glutton for punishment in relationships, then consider baking the glutton's reward.

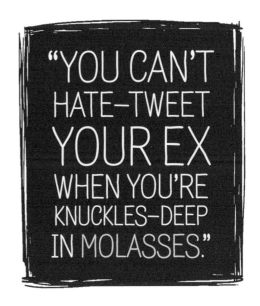

"YOU CAN'T HATE-TWEET YOUR EX WHEN YOU'RE KNUCKLES-DEEP IN MOLASSES."

Yeah, yeah . . . blah, blah, blah . . . You didn't crack the spine of this book for some keep-your-hands-in-the-cookie-dough,stay-busy-and-stay-happy type of sage advice. You came here to, well, crack some spines, right? You came here for one thing and one thing only: R-E-V-E-N-G-E.

And that's exactly what you're gonna get.

You see, there are two types of SWEET REVENGE — and, not coincidentally, two ways to use this book.

Option #1: *Instead of the high road, take the pie road.*

These two things are basically one and the same. It's a best-foot-forward, lemon-squares-out-of-lemons, gray-skies-are-gonna-clear-up-so-put-on-a-happy-face way of thinking. A smile-to-their-face and then stab-'em-in-the back mentality.

Now some people might say this type of passive-aggressive nature isn't healthy. That if you keep bottling up, swallowing all your emotions, they'll eventually — KA-BOOM!! — explode like a two-ton atom bomb, rippling through through your Twitter feed and singeing the filtered dog-nose whiskers off your Snapchat followers.

SWEET REVENGE isn't about bottling up your feelings. The opposite, in fact. SWEET REVENGE is about taking all your bittersweet memories, mixing in a little flour and sugar, and creating something delicious out of them. Then, once and for all, gifting away your over-mixed emotions and half-baked anger to those who truly deserve them: your enemies & exes.

WERKIN

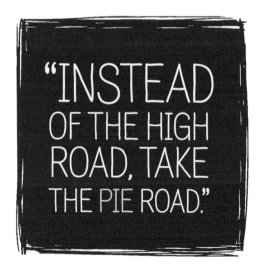

"INSTEAD OF THE HIGH ROAD, TAKE THE PIE ROAD."

Don't get me wrong. . . . Letting go of them is tough. But then again, when is sharing a dessert ever easy?

Option #2: *The best revenge is eating well.*

Forget sharing. Just make the things in this book and, well, EAT THEM. That's right — treat yo-self! Bake the You're the Devil Food Cake (page 70) and EAT IT. Make the Go Fudge Yourself (page 152) and EAT IT. Mix up some When I Think of Us, Ice Cream (page 172) and (you guessed it . . .) EAT IT! EAT ALL THE THINGS. And post pics of yourself doing it! Show him or her or whoever that you don't need him or her or whoever. You need food, and that's it (and, technically, water and air . . .). Nothing else!

In other words, grab life by the milk balls, and eat the crap out of it — because, fyi, it's too sweet to waste.

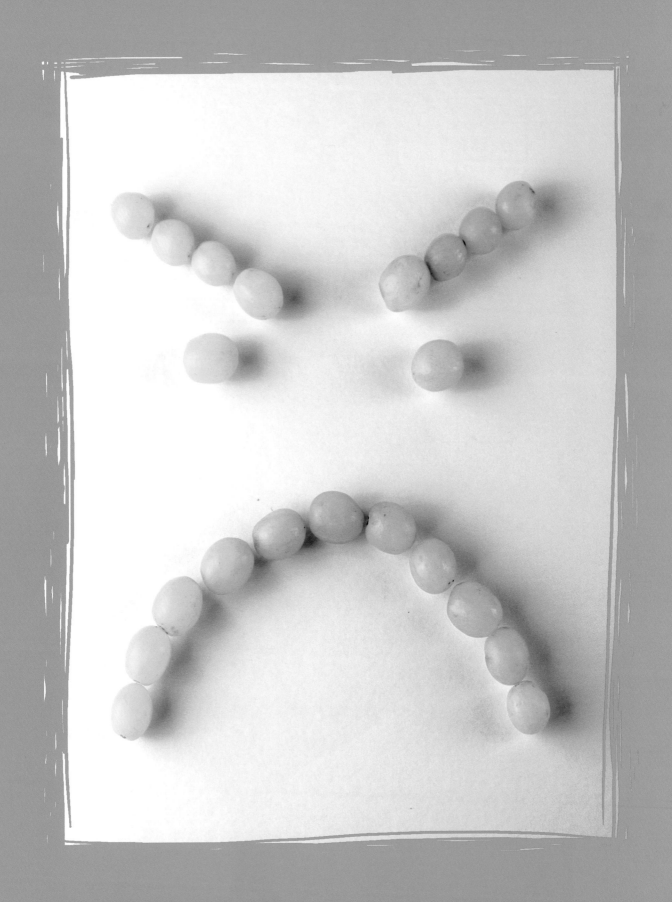

100% TOTALLY ESSENTIAL TOOLS OF
SWEET *REVENGE*

BLOWTORCH
(fire! fire!)

FRYING PAN
(cast iron, imho)

MALLET
(aka MEAT
TENDERIZER)

BUTCHER KNIFE (preferably razor-sharp)

ROLLING PIN (the heavier, the better)

PLASTIC WRAP (clearly)

OK, THOSE THINGS ARE ONLY, LIKE, 10% ESSENTIAL, BUT THESE ARE PRETTY IMPORTANT:

Mixing bowls (tiny, medium-ish, big ol')

Measuring cups/spoons

Baking sheets

Cake/cupcake pans

Saucepans

Electric mixer

Rubber spatula

Whisk

Spoons

Cookie scoops

Thermometer

Parchment paper/Silpat®

Microwave

Oven (or an open fire)

Coffee

Coffee

Coffee . . .

LEGEND(ARY)

BURNS

In SWEET REVENGE, the level of burn to be delivered = the degree of recipe difficulty. Say you bake a simple cupcake — that's a mild burn. But spend 8 hrs on a 15-layer cake . . . EPIC.

MILD
Little effort. Like a spring-break sunburn.

1ST DEGREE
Some difficulty: Ooh . . . That's gonna blister.

2ND DEGREE
Getting harder. Better stock up on aloe, y'all.

EPIC
The tough stuff. Spontaneous-combustion level burnage.

REVENGE
If you're gonna count your blessings, you might as well count your revenges.

SERVINGS
*Average servings — does not include rage-eating an entire chocolate cake (which is totally acceptable, btw).

BAKE TIME
In love, timing is everything. Same goes for baking.

HACKS
Follow Spatula Bunny's tips & hacks, and all your desserts will have hoppy endings. :)

CONVERSIONS

"It's gettin' hot in here!"

Fahrenheit (°F)	Celsius (°C)
450°	230°
425°	220°
400°	200°
375°	190°
350°	180°
325°	160°

1/4 teaspoon	1.25 grams or milliliters
1/2 teaspoon	2.5 g or mL
1 teaspoon	5 g or mL
1 tablespoon	15 g or mL
1/4 cup	57 g (dry) or 60 mL (liquid)
1/3 cup	75 g (dry) or 80 mL (liquid)
1/2 cup	114 g (dry) or 125 mL (liquid)
2/3 cup	150 g (dry) or 160 mL (liquid)
3/4 cup	170 g (dry) or 175 mL (liquid)
1 cup	227 g (dry) or 240 mL (liquid)
1 quart	950 mL

GO AHEAD AND *BITE ME-* SIZED TREATS

COOKIES, BARS & BALLS

WHAT A TOTAL MONSTER

AKA:

CAP'N CRUNCH® MONSTER COOKIES

You can't always judge a cookie — or a partner — by their oh-so-beautiful, ooey-gooey deliciousness. Because that doesn't mean they aren't filled with a monster-load of crap. In baking, that's A-OK. In an S.O. or a best friend, not so much.

EAT ME.

1 cup butter, room temp
1 cup granulated sugar
2/3 cup brown sugar
1 tablespoon corn syrup
1 egg
1 tablespoon heavy cream
1 teaspoon vanilla extract
1 2/3 cup all-purpose flour
1/2 teaspoon baking powder
1/8 teaspoon baking soda
1 tablespoon salt
2/3 cup mini chocolate chips
1 cup M&M's® chocolate candies
2/3 cup graham cracker crumbs
2/3 cup old-fashioned oats
2/3 cup cornmeal
1 tablespoon milk powder
4 snack-size bags Nacho Cheese Doritos®
1 cup Cap'n Crunch®

i.e., Not melted, OK?

Junk food bonanza!

HACK IT

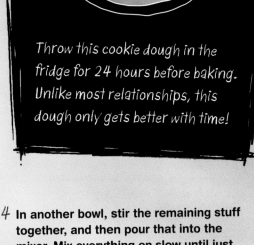

Throw this cookie dough in the fridge for 24 hours before baking. Unlike most relationships, this dough only gets better with time!

1 Crank up your oven to 375°F.

2 In a large-ish mixing bowl, paddle the butter, both sugars, and corn syrup on medium speed for about 5 minutes. Then scrape down the bowl.

3 Dump in the egg, heavy cream, and vanilla extract. Paddle on medium speed for another 8 minutes or so. Scrape down that bowl again.

4 In another bowl, stir the remaining stuff together, and then pour that into the mixer. Mix everything on slow until just incorporated. Do not overmix, you guys.

5 Plop spoonfuls of that delicious AF cookie dough onto a parchment- or Silpat®-lined baking sheet, 2 inches apart. Bake 'em up for about 18 minutes, turning the sheet halfway through.

6 Remove from the oven when the cookies are golden and set in the centers and you just can't wait anymore. Cool on the sheet for 1 minute (cheaters never win), and then move them to a rack or flip upside down to cool all the way.

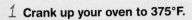

CHEW ON THIS

Made for nonstick cooking, a Silpat® silicone rubber mat is everything when working w/ sticky stuff, like gooey batter, taffy, caramel, dough, etc.

KISS MY *MOLASSES*

AKA:

MOLASSES GINGERSNAPS W/ LEMON CURD

Truth: Without the sour, life just isn't as sweet. Sure, one relationship or friendship might end up a complete and utter curd. But the next? Well, it just might be as sweet & sticky as molasses.

PUCKER UP!

GINGERSNAPS

1 cup granulated sugar

2 cups all-purpose flour

2 teaspoons baking soda

1/2 teaspoon salt

1 tablespoon dried ginger powder

1 teaspoon cinnamon

3/4 cup vegetable shortening

1 egg

1/4 cup dark molasses

As opposed to LIGHT molasses — duh!

1/3 cup sugar in the raw

1 Flip on your oven to 350°F.

2 In medium bowl, whisk all the dry ingredients together. Set that stuff aside.

3 In a larger mixing bowl, mix vegetable shortening and sugar together until oh-so fluffy. Then dump in the egg, molasses, and dry ingredients, and mix together.

4 Shape dough into 1-inch balls, roll in the sugar in the raw, and then plop 'em 2 inches apart on an ungreased baking sheet. *(Do NOT flatten those little suckers!)*

5 Bake for about 7 minutes, and then turn the sheet and bake another 5 minutes or so.

6 Remove them from the oven when the edges are firm and the centers are tummy-soft. Cool on the sheet for 1 minute, and then move to a rack and cool all the way.

LEMON CURD

1/2 cup lemon juice

1/2 cup granulated sugar

2 large egg yolks

2 large eggs

1/2 teaspoon salt

6 tablespoons butter

1 Place a fine mesh strainer over a medium bowl and set aside.

2 In another bowl, whisk together the lemon juice, sugar, egg yolks, eggs, and salt. Set aside.

3 Melt butter in a medium saucepan over low heat. Then crank the heat to medium and add the lemon-juice mixture, whisking until that stuff thickens into a pudding. *Mmm... pudding*

4 Take off heat and smash that curd through the mesh strainer. Throw it in the fridge until cooled.

TO ASSEMBLE:

Dunk plain cookies directly into a bowlful of the curd, or make cookie & curd sandwiches. (Heck yeah!)

HACK IT

No cooling rack? No worries. Let those bad boys set a couple minutes. Then flip 'em upside down on the same sheet. BOOM! Problem solved.

OH, SNAP...BONUS!

SOFT GINGER–MOLASSES COOKIES W/ LEMON ICING

COOKIES

3/4 cup coconut oil

1 cup granulated sugar

1 egg, beaten

1/4 cup dark molasses

2 cups all-purpose flour

2 teaspoons baking soda

1/2 teaspoon salt

1 tablespoon ginger

1 teaspoon cinnamon

To coat:

1/3 cup demerara sugar

A raw, large-grained, golden-amber sugar. Basically edible Pixie Dust.

1 Crank oven to 350°F.

2 In a big bowl, mix coconut oil and sugar until creamy & dreamy.

3 Dump in that egg and then the molasses. Then add the remaining stuff and mix until all's nice and cozy.

4 Shape dough into 1-inch balls, and then roll them in the demerara sugar.

5 Bake on an ungreased baking sheet for about 10 minutes or until cookies are set.

ICING

4 cups powdered sugar

3 tablespoons lemon juice (tweak for preferred smoothness)

Pinch of salt

1 In a just-right bowl, stir the ingredients until smooth.

2 Spread icing onto cookies with a butter knife or spoon or photos of your exes & enemies. :)

(kidding–not-kidding)

> IN FOOD AND RELATIONSHIPS, I'M GREEDY SOMETIMES. I WANT IT ALL. LIKE EVERYONE SHOULD.

EAT MY WORDS

SUGAR PROFILES

You know what they say, variety is the spice of life. Well, it's the sugar of life too. So don't settle for just one. Get out there and play the field — the sugarcane field, that is. :)

Granulated
Super-white & average

Hobbies: I love just about everything . . . including you. ;)

Quote: "I might not be the sexiest sugar around, but when it comes to reliability, I take the cake — and can bake in one too!"

Powdered
Fine as heck & high-maintenance

Hobbies: Cake decorating & dusting

Quote: "I'm not a fan of dirty work. (In fact, dusting is my favorite pastime!) But I'll be the icing on your cake any day."

Turbinado
Raw & unrefined

Hobbies: Drinking (in coffee, mostly)

Quote: "No comment."

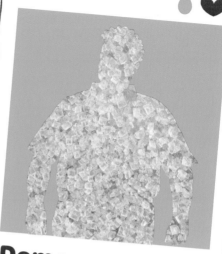

Demerara
Big ol' sweetheart

Hobbies: Being a big ol' sweetheart

Quote: "When it comes to sweetness — size matters."

Sanding
A bit of a showoff

Hobbies: Sparkling & twinkling & being oh-so fabulous

Quote: "Is that a twinkle in your eye, or is that just me shining like a friggin' star?"

Brown
Dark & mysterious & hella-rich

Hobbies: Baking & making sauces & glazes

Quote: "Just turn up the heat, baby, and I'll melt like butta."

!#$&%!!

I HONESTLY DON'T GIVE A

FIG

AKA:

FIGGY COOKIES

Light, flaky, and oh-so figa-licious, these cookies are edible childhood. So why not gift them to the most immature ex or enemy in your life? And for extra funsies, cut them into alphabet shapes! Like, F or U or some other random, not meaningful-at-all letters. Now doesn't that feel good?

!#$&%!!

DOUGH

1 cup granulated sugar

1/2 cup butter, room temp

1 large egg

1 tablespoon heavy cream

1/2 teaspoon vanilla extract

1/2 teaspoon salt

1 teaspoon baking powder

1 3/4 cups all-purpose flour

FILLING

1 10–12-ounce jar fig jam

1 For the dough, whisk together the sugar, butter, egg, heavy cream, and vanilla extract until wonderfully blended. Then dump in the dry ingredients and mix well.

2 Stick this dough in the fridge for about an hour.

3 Crank the oven to 350°F.

4 Split the dough in half, and then roll out both dough halves to 1/4-inch thick or so.

5 Line a 13 x 9-inch baking dish with the first half of dough. Using a butter knife or spatula *(or diary entries about your frenemies)*, evenly spread out fig jam on top. Then cover the jam with the second half of the dough.

6 Bake that figginess for about 30 minutes, turning once halfway through.

7 Cool completely and cut into preferred shapes.

(or burn the crap out of your mouth...)

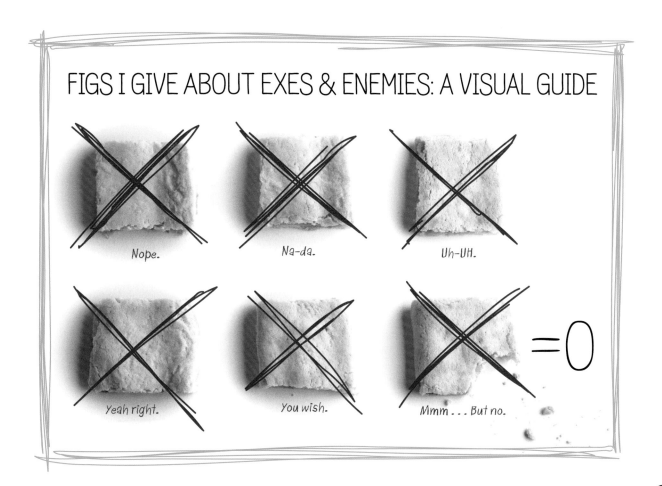

FIGS I GIVE ABOUT EXES & ENEMIES: A VISUAL GUIDE

Nope.

Na-da.

Uh-UH.

Yeah right.

You wish.

Mmm . . . But no.   =0

THE BAR HAS BEEN LOWERED

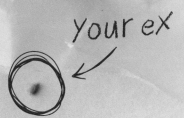

THE BAR

AKA:

CHOCOLATE-HAZELNUT PEANUT BUTTER BARS

Before that one relationship, you had high expectations. You set the bar pretty high — like Chocolate-Hazelnut Peanut Butter Bars high. Now? Heck, you barely expect to lick the spoon. Well don't give up! Expect Chocolate-Hazelnut Peanut Butter Bars. Always.

your ex

38

1/2 cup butter, softened

1/2 cup peanut butter

1 cup brown sugar

1 egg

1 teaspoon of vanilla extract

1 cup all-purpose flour

1/3 cup chocolate-hazelnut spread

1 Get your oven rolling to 350°F.

2 Grease up an 8 x 8-inch baking pan with butter (yay!) or nonstick cooking spray (eh).

3 In a medium bowl, mix the butter and peanut butter using a rubber spatula until fluffy. Scrape down sides of bowl.

4 Dump in brown sugar, mixing until all's together. Scrape down sides.

5 Crack in an egg, and then add vanilla, and mix again until incorporated. (Yep, scrape down those sides again.)

6 Mix in flour until moist, and ←EW! then pour that mixture into the baking pan.

7 Drop the chocolate-hazelnut spread by spoonfuls into the pan. Using the back of a spoon, swirl it into the peanut-butter mixture. (Rotate swirl patterns clockwise and counterclockwise for funsies!)

8 Bake that gooeyness for about 30 minutes or until center is set and sides are goldened.

9 Cool completely and cut into squares or circles or broken hearts or whatever.

No, wait...THIS is your ex.

WORLD'S BIGGEST *FLAKE*

AKA:
BUTTERFINGER® FLAKE BARS

(TOP VIEW) ↙

These simple, no-bake treats are simply unforgettable. Even for a total flake, who would pretty much forget anything. Like a birthday. Or an anniversary. Or you at the zoo, when they left to take a leak, never came back, and you were stuck with the GD gorillas for three and a half hours. (Or, you know, something like that . . .)

BASE

1 16-ounce jar creamy peanut butter

1 cup dark chocolate chips

1/4 cup butter

1 cup of Butterfinger®, crushed

3 cups rice flakes cereal, crushed

1/4 cup cocoa nibs

1 tablespoon salt

TOPPING

2/3 cup heavy cream

1 teaspoon vanilla extract

1 cup butterscotch chips

1 cup white chocolate chips

1 tablespoon kosher salt

1/2 cup of granulated sugar

3 tablespoon butter

A fancy-pants term for browning sugar w/ heat

1 Butter up a quarter-size sheet pan and line with Silpat® or parchment paper. Set aside.

2 In a medium saucepan, melt the peanut butter, chocolate chips, and butter over low heat. Then remove from heat and stir in the Butterfinger®, cereal, cocoa nibs, and salt.

3 Dump that mixture onto the prepped sheet pan, pressing firmly until mixture is solid, like a grade-A Rice Krispies Treat®.

4 Chill that goodness to at least room temp.

5 Meanwhile, for the topping, (scald) cream and vanilla in a small saucepan. Set aside.

(Bring nearly to a boil and then cool down.)

6 Place butterscotch chips, white chocolate chips, and salt in a medium-ish bowl and set a strainer over the top.

7 In a separate saucepan, (caramelize) the sugar until it starts to smoke and froth like a rabid dog. Remove from heat and immediately add butter, stirring until totally incorporated.

8 Pour this mixture over the strainer and onto the butterscotch and white chocolate chips.

9 Add scalded cream and vanilla to that and stir everything up.

10 Immediately spread this deliciousness over the base until evenly distributed.

11 Chill and top with additional crushed Butterfinger®, if desired.

(Um, yes please!)

Cut bars into single-serve pieces:

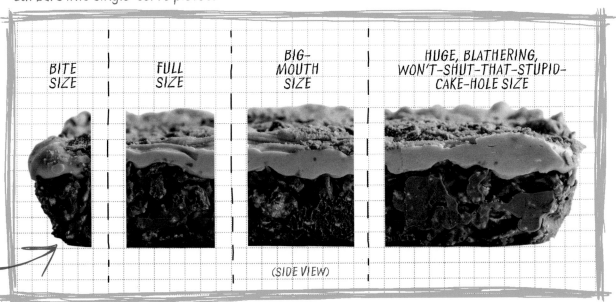

BITE SIZE

FULL SIZE

BIG-MOUTH SIZE

HUGE, BLATHERING, WON'T-SHUT-THAT-STUPID-CAKE-HOLE SIZE

(SIDE VIEW)

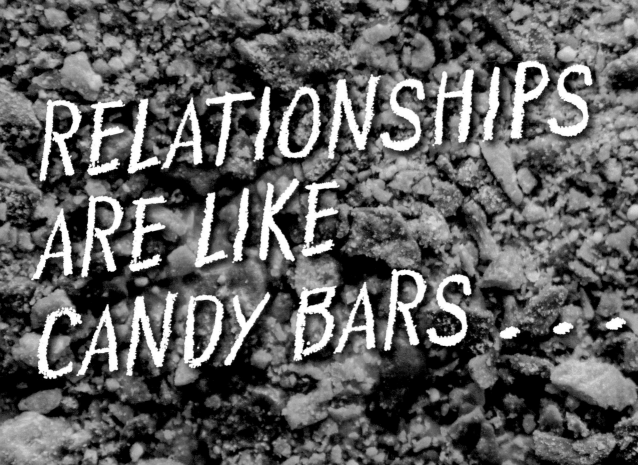

SWEET, NUTTY, AND FULL OF REGRET.

IT TAKES A *LATTE* BALLS

AKA:

PUMPKIN–SPICE LATTE BALLS W/ CHEX MIX® CRUMBLE

BALLS IT TAKES*:

1 2 3

4 5 6

7 8 9

*Not pictured: a lot more balls.

Dumping an S.O. or unfriending a BFF takes balls. Maybe you had all the right ingredients, the perfect amount of heat, and even semidecent timing. Still, the final results left a bitter taste in your mouth. Well, don't worry. The cookbook of life has more than one recipe, folks. So try another! Like these deliciously spicy, no-bake balls that — BONUS! — are guaranteed not to burn you again.

CRUMBLE

1 teaspoon cinnamon

2 tablespoons granulated sugar

1 cup Chocolate Chex Mix®, crumbled

1 packet instant coffee

(or 1 heaping teaspoon)

BALLS

2/3 cup coconut oil, room temp

1/2 cup granulated sugar

1/2 cup pumpkin pie filling

1/4 cup peanut butter

1 teaspoon vanilla extract

1/4 teaspoon salt

1 packet instant coffee

1 teaspoon cinnamon

3/4 cup coconut flour

1/2 cup sweet white rice flour

Fresh nutmeg, grated

1 **Dump all the Chex Mix® crumble ingredients into a gallon-sized, resealable plastic bag.** *Shake it like a Polaroid picture,* **and then set that shook-up crunchiness aside.**

2 **In a medium-ish bowl, whip up the coconut oil and sugar until fluffy and smooth and oh-so heavenly.**

3 **Mix in the remaining ball ingredients until totally integrated.**

4 **Scoop and shape dough into 1-inch truffle balls or** *about the size of your ex's or enemy's brain.*

ZING!

5 **Place 1–2 truffle balls into the bag of Chex Mix® crumble. Gently shake the bag until balls are completely coated. Repeat with all balls.**

6 **Stick those balls in the fridge for about an hour or until totally chilled out.**

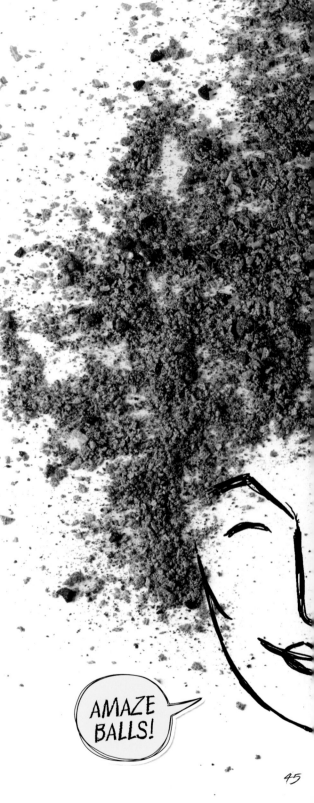

AMAZE BALLS!

NOBODY'S *BUTTER CUP*

AKA:

PRETZEL-PEANUT-BUTTER CUPS

Ever get gum stuck in your hair? Um . . . me neither. Well, I've heard *winks* it's a real headache. It sticks and pulls and clings like a needy ex or enemy. Besides cutting your hair, there's only one thing that works: peanut butter. The moral? Don't change for some chewed-up, spit-out wad. Because PEANUT BUTTER.

...OR THEIR HONEY...

...OR THEIR SUGAR...

...OR THEIR SWEETIE...

...OR THEIR CUPCAKE...

1/2 cup pretzels, crushed

1 1/4 cup (semisweet) chocolate chips

3/4 cup creamy peanut butter

1/4 cup powdered sugar

1/2 teaspoon vanilla extract

1/4 teaspoon kosher salt

More cocoa sugar deep flavor!

1 Line a 24-cup mini muffin pan with cupcake wrappers. Then evenly distribute the crushed pretzels between those cute little cups.

See next page!

2 Melt the semisweet chocolate chips over a (double boiler) on the stove or nuke that stuff in the microwave.

3 Once melted, dump a teaspoon of chocolate into each itty-bitty cup.

4 In a small-ish bowl, stir the peanut butter, powdered sugar, vanilla extract, and salt. Then dump this mixture into a plastic sandwich baggie.

5 Cut a corner of the baggie and (pipe) the mixture into the center of each muffin cup.

Squeeze until it squirts out.

6 Pour the remaining melted chocolate over the cups, and then throw it in the fridge till cooled.

A TRULY AMICABLE SPLIT

SLICE ME OFF A
PIECE OF THAT

A totally incomplete & not-at-all comprehensive list of food-related terms of objectification*:

APPLE OF MY EYE	LAMBCHOP
ARM CANDY	LOVE MUFFIN
BABYCAKES	MUFFIN
BEEFCAKE	PEACH
BONBON	PEACHY PIE
BUTTERCUP	PEANUT
BUTTERSCOTCH	PICKLE PIE
CAKES	PINEAPPLE CHUNK
CHUNKY MONKEY	POP TART
COOKIE	PORK CHOP
CREAM PUFF	PUDDIN'
CUDDLE CAKES	PUDDIN' POP
CUDDLE MUFFIN	PUMPKIN
CUPCAKE	PUMPKIN BUTT
CUTIE PIE	SHORT CAKE
DUMPLING	SNICKERDOODLE
EYE CANDY	STUD MUFFIN
GUMDROP	SUGAR
GUMMY BEAR	SUGAR DADDY
HONEY	SUGAR PIE
HONEY BABY	SUGAR PLUM
HONEY BUNNY	SUGAR LIPS
HONEY CAKES	SWEET CHEEKS
HONEY BEAR	SWEET PEA
HONEYBUN	SWEETHEART
HONEYBUNCH	SWEETIE PIE
HONEYBUNS	SWEETSTUFF
HOT TAMALE	TATOR-TOT
KIT KAT	TWINKIE

*i.e., things no one should call you . . . unless you want them to!

MELT MY HEART

Let's be honest, only one thing can truly make you melt . . . CHOCOLATE! Like, you're totally ready to ask for its melt-in-your-mouth-not-In-your hand in marriage, and finally take that metaphorical plunge into the chocolate fountain of life, amirite?

Well, slow your nut-roll! Because, like in any relationship, good things only come to those who wait. So here are two ways to keep you and your chocolate-love from getting burned (again).

№1: GO NUKE–LEAR

Chop chocolate bars into small pieces (or use chips, ya slacker). Place in a glass, microwave-safe bowl and nuke at 50% for 2 minutes or so. Stir and repeat, if necessary.

№2: DOUBLE DOWN

Hack a double boiler by placing a heatproof glass bowl over a pot of simmering water, making sure the water doesn't touch the bottom of the bowl. Stir in chocolate pieces or chips until ultra-smooth.

8

I CANNOLI BE HAPPY WHEN WE'RE THROUGH!

AKA:

CANNOLI WAFFLES

(DONE!
DONZO!
FORSHUNZO!
FINISHED!
FINITO!
OVER!
TERMINATED!
KAPUT!
HISTORY!
SPLITSVILLE!
DEAD & BURIED!
PAST!
NOTHING!)

20

They say "parting is such sweet sorrow," but sometimes it's just really sweet.
Like these rich, creamy cannoli, the perfect parting gift to a former frenemy.
Because, after all, you don't actually wish them the worst. Just not the best.

2 cups all-purpose flour

1 1/3 tablespoons baking powder

1/2 teaspoon salt

1/4 cup granulated sugar

2 eggs, separated

2 cups whole milk

1/2 teaspoon vanilla extract

1/2 cup vegetable oil

HACK IT

Ain't got time for that? Fyi, toaster waffles work in a pinch.

1 Mix all the dry ingredients together in a medium bowl. Set that aside.

2 In another bowl, beat those egg whites until fluffy and stiff.

3 In *ANOTHER* large bowl, mix the egg yolks, milk, vanilla, and oil.

4 Add dry-ingredient mixture into the large bowl of wet ingredients and mix well.

5 Gently fold in beaten egg whites, maintaining all that fluffiness.

6 Cook the waffle batter according to waffle-iron instructions.

Tip: Recruit someone else to do the dishes and repay them w/ sweets!

FILLING

3/4 cup powdered sugar

1 teaspoon ground cinnamon

1 cup mascarpone cheese

1 cup ricotta cheese

1/4 cup heavy cream

Lemon zest, grated *(yellow part only!)*

Fresh nutmeg, grated

1/4 cup small, semisweet chocolate chips

1 In a big bowl, whisk together the sugar, cinnamon, and mascarpone and ricotta cheeses until silky-smooth.

2 In a separate mixing bowl, beat the heavy cream until stiffened.

3 Using a rubber spatula, gently fold cream into ricotta mixture, maintaining fluffiness.

4 Stir in chocolate chips, lemon zest, and nutmeg. Then throw it in the fridge for about 1–1 1/2 hours.

Now get crackin' (i.e., turn the page)! →

QUIZ: SHOULD I SAY "BUH–BYE" TO MY EX AND/OR ENEMY?

Answer these 3 questions for a 100% definitive decision.

1. ARE YOU READING THIS QUIZ?

☐ YES ☐ NO

2. ARE YOU READING THIS QUIZ?

☐ YES ☐ NO

3. ARE YOU READING THIS QUIZ?

☐ YES ☐ NO

If you answered YES to any or all these questions, say "buh-bye." Because life = too short.

CANDIED PISTACHIOS

1 cup granulated sugar

1 cup pistachios, shelled

Salt, to taste

1 **Spread a single layer of pistachios onto a parchment- or Silpat®-lined baking sheet. Set aside.**

2 **On the stovetop, add an even layer of sugar to a nonstick saucepan or skillet. Melt sugar, continuously stirring with a rubber spatula, until golden-amber.** *(Not brown!)* **If sugar burns, discard and try again!**

3 **Immediately pour melted sugar over pistachios and sprinkle with salt.**

(Do not touch until cooled — sugar burns suck!)

4 **Once cooled and hardened, break candied pistachios into tiny pieces.** *(Place in a large, resealable plastic bag, cover with a towel, and beat the living daylights out of it with rolling pin or brass knuckles or whatever.)*

CHOCOLATE–COFFEE SAUCE

1 cup semisweet mini chocolate chips

2 tablespoons corn syrup

1 cup heavy cream

1 packet *(or 1 heaping teaspoon)* **instant coffee**

Pinch of salt

1 **On stovetop, mix all the ingredients into a medium saucepan over low heat. Whisk continuously until melted and totally incorporated.**

TO ASSEMBLE:

1. **Sandwich cold cannoli filling between two hot waffles.**

2. **Sprinkle with candied pistachios and drizzle chocolate coffee sauce on top.**

9

EVERY DAY I REGRET US
S'MORE

AKA:

S'MORE BROWNIES

Ah, s'mores . . . Sugary-sweet, ooey-gooey, perfectly packaged nostalgia. Reminders of late-night campfires, cookouts, and *shudder* an ex. Ok, listen up: you can regret a former S.O. or ex-friend, but please don't regret a dessert. Someone left a bad taste in your mouth? So what. Take all that and make something better — like a twist on a summertime classic or a no-regrets, kick-butt life.

OH, BURN!

MARSHMALLOWS

3 packages unflavored gelatin

1 cup icy-cold water, divided

1 1/2 cups granulated sugar

1 cup light corn syrup

1/4 teaspoon kosher salt

1 teaspoon vanilla extract

1/4 cup powdered sugar

1/4 cup cornstarch

Butter or nonstick cooking spray

SWEETHEARTS ARE GREAT. BUT SO ARE CREAMY, NUTTY, SALTY-HEARTS TOO.

EAT MY WORDS

1 **Bloom** *(a fancy-schmancy term for "soak that stuff")* gelatin in a medium-ish stand-mixer bowl, along with 1/2 cup of water.

2 **In a small saucepan, cook remaining 1/2 cup water, sugar, corn syrup, and salt over medium heat until mixture reaches 240°F. Remove from the heat.**

3 **Turn the stand mixer on low, and slowly pour the sugar-syrup into that bloomed-up gelatin.**

4 **Crank up the speed to high, whipping until mixture becomes thick, glossy-white, and lukewarm (about 12–15 minutes or so).**

5 **Dump in vanilla and whip another additional minute. Turn off stand mixer. Set aside.**

6 **In another bowl, whisk together powdered sugar and cornstarch.**

7 **Butter up (or spray down) a 13 x 9-inch baking pan, and then coat bottom and sides of pan with 1/3 of the powdered-sugar mix.**

8 **Using a rubber spatula, scrape marshmallow mixture into a coated pan. Spray spatula with nonstick cooking spray to avoid sticking.**

9 **Sprinkle remaining powdered-sugar mixture on top.**

10 **Cure marshmallows at room temp, allowing them to sit uncovered for at least 4 hours and up to overnight.**

11 **Once cured, flip marshmallows onto a cutting board, lightly dusted with powdered-sugar mixture. Using a knife or cookie cutter, cut into desired shapes.** *(May I suggest broken hearts?)*

12 **Dust all sides of each marshmallow with remaining powdered-sugar mixture.**

HACK IT

Give your marshmallows wicked flavor with dried lavender, cocoa powder, or — wait for it — powdered Tang®!

Hehe
FIRE!
FIRE!
FIRE!

STREUSEL

3 graham cracker squares, crumbled

1/4 cup brown sugar, packed

1/8 teaspoon ground cinnamon

2 tablespoons butter, melted

1 teaspoon vanilla extract

2 tablespoons granulated sugar

1/2 teaspoon salt

1 **In a small bowl, combine ingredients** *using fingers* **until mixture resembles big crumbs.**

(If you're the squeamish, eats-popcorn-with-chopsticks type, feel free to combine using a fork.)

BROWNIES

10 tablespoons butter

1 1/4 cups granulated sugar

1 cup, unsweetened cocoa powder

1 packet *(or 1 heaping teaspoon)* **instant coffee**

1/4 teaspoon salt

1 teaspoon vanilla extract

2 large eggs

1/2 cup flour

1. Flip on your oven to 325°F.

2. Line bottom and sides of an 8 x 8-inch baking pan with parchment paper or foil, letting the extra stuff overhang on all sides.

3. On stovetop, mix the butter, sugar, cocoa powder, coffee, and salt in a midsized saucepan on low heat, until the butter has melted and mixture is warm.

4. Remove this stuff from the heat and stir in vanilla extract. Then crack in the eggs, one at a time, whisking after each one. Then dump in the flour and stir until totally incorporated.

5. Pour mixture into the prepped pan and spread evenly. Bake 20–25 minutes or until a toothpick (or chopstick!) inserted into the center comes out almost clean. *(to avoid certain death)*

6. (Cool completely,) and then lift from pan using the excess parchment paper or foil. (You remembered to do that, right?) Place onto cookie sheet.

TO ASSEMBLE:

Top brownies with marshmallows, and then sprinkle with graham streusel. Carefully torch or broil marshmallows until golden brown and streusel is lightly crunchy.

HOW TO PACKAGE GIFTS FOR AN ENEMY

IN A FLAMING PAPER BAG
(Too cliche)

VIA SNAIL MAIL
(Too slow)

INSIDE A SWEATY FIST
(Too messy)

IN A SHOE BOX FULL OF BAD MEMORIES
(Too painful)

ATOP A HEAPING PILE OF TRASH
(Too stinky)

IN A BOX WITH A BOW
(Perfectly passive aggressive!)

FORGETTING YOU WAS A

PIECE OF CAKE

CAKES & CUPCAKES

10

I COULDN'T *CARROT* ALL CAKE

AKA:

CARROT CAKE TRUFFLES
W/ COOL RANCH DORITOS® SUGAR

What? You think carrot cake and tortilla chips are a weird combo? Let me tell you something, folks: carrot cake is already pretty frickin' weird. I mean, carrots and cake? Even the name is an oxymoron. You know, like, "jumbo shrimp" or "freezer burn" or "ex boyfriends & girlfriends." Oh wait — those last ones . . . they're just morons.

CAKE

1 1/2 cups all-purpose flour

1 cup granulated sugar

1 1/2 teaspoons baking soda

1 teaspoon baking powder

2 teaspoons cinnamon

1/2 teaspoon ground cloves

1/2 teaspoon nutmeg

1/2 teaspoon ginger, grated

1/2 teaspoon salt

2/3 cup vegetable oil

3 large eggs, beaten

1 1/2 cups carrots, peeled and finely grated

1 Crank the oven to 350°F.

2 In a big bowl, whisk together the flour, sugar, baking soda, baking powder, and spices until totally combined.

3 Stir in oil and those beaten-up eggs. Then, dump in the carrots and stir again until ingredients are all together and harmonious and beautiful.

4 With a rubber spatula, scrape that batter into a 9 x 13-inch cake pan, spreading evenly.

5 Bake for 30–35 minutes or until a toothpick or hair bobby or friend-turned-enemy friendship bracelet inserted into the center comes out clean as a whistle. *(Btw, why are whistles always clean?)*

6 Allow that cake to cool, and then cut it into large cubes.

7 Place cubes into a food processor and pulse until cake is completely crumbled.

(Or just smoosh the crap out of it w/ your hands and skip all this mechanical nonsense!)

Like... WHATEVS.

FROSTING

4 ounces cream cheese, room temp

1/2 cup butter, room temp

2 cups powdered sugar

1 teaspoon vanilla extract

1/2 teaspoon salt

1 In a large-ish mixing bowl, whip the cream cheese and butter until light and fluffy and oh-so heavenly. Scrape down the sides of the bowl with a rubber spatula.

2 Slooooowly add the powdered sugar, then vanilla and salt, whipping until fluffy. (Yep, and scrape down the sides of the bowl again.)

I declare this... Peak Nacho!

COOL RANCH DORITOS® SUGAR

1 cup Cool Ranch Doritos®, crumbled
(PRO TIP: Consume remaining contents of bag.)

1/2 cup granulated sugar

1 **In a tiny bowl, mix crumbled Cool Ranch Doritos® and sugar until combined.**

TO ASSEMBLE:

1. **Fold carrot cake crumbles into frosting mixture with a rubber spatula, blending until well incorporated.**

2. **Using a small cookie scoop** *(or, you know, handsies)***, scoop cake mixture into truffle balls.**

3. **Gently roll truffle balls, one by one, in Cool Ranch Doritos® Sugar, coating until deliciously dusted.**

WANNA BE A STRAIGHT-UP BALLER?

Sick of striking out . . . in the kitchen? Here's a couple ways to seriously up your ball-game.

№1:

GET HANDSY

Sleek, sexy new toys & gadgets (i.e., cookie scoops) might turn you on, but when it comes to the perfect cookie balls, go au naturel. That's right — get your digits in there. Take 2 tablespoons of dough and gently roll between both hands before placing on a cookie sheet. Oooh yeah . . .

№2:

LUBE UP

Never put yourself in a, um, sticky situation. Take preventative measures — like flouring or spraying your hands with nonstick cooking oil — to avoid an unwanted mess.

№3:

COOL THINGS DOWN

Things getting too hot & heavy? Don't be afraid to cool things down. Throw your dough in the fridge for 15 minutes, making it easier to shape and form into balls.

11

YOU'RE THE *DEVIL FOOD CAKE*

AKA:

DEVIL'S FOOD CAKE W/ CHOCOLATE FROSTING & BROWNIE-STREUSEL CRUNCH

Expectation: Knight in Shining Armor.
Reality: Prince(ss) of Darkness.
This sinfully delicious cake is perfect
for an old flame (i.e., Hell's Spawn).
Best eaten with a pitchfork.

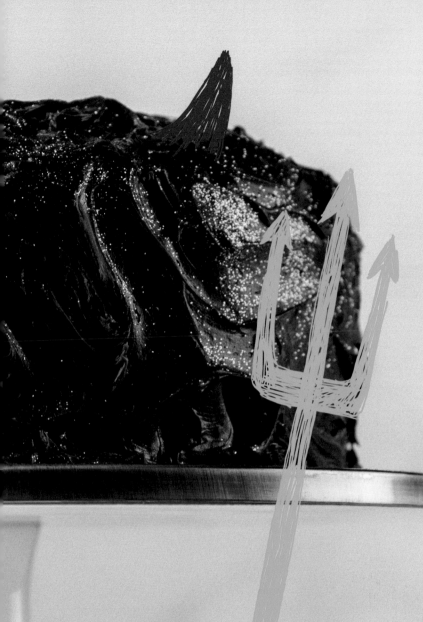

CAKE

3/4 cup cocoa powder *(or water — but REALLY?!)*

3/4 cup coffee

4 ounces of semisweet chocolate chips

2 cups all-purpose flour

1 1/2 teaspoons baking soda

1/4 teaspoon kosher salt

12 tablespoons butter, softened

2 cups granulated sugar

5 eggs

1 cup milk

1 Get that oven rolling to 350°F.

2 Butter up two round, 9-inch cake pans, and then line the bottoms of the pans with parchment paper.

3 In a small-ish bowl, stir cocoa powder with coffee *(or water if you prefer, but again, WHY?)*, forming a paste. Set aside.

4 Nuke the chocolate in a microwave, separately.

5 In another bowl, mix up the flour, baking soda, and salt.

6 In a big ol' mixing bowl, beat butter and sugar until pale and fluffy *(and you've expelled all your pent-up rage)*. **Stir in eggs, one at a time. Then, dump in the cocoa paste and melted chocolate, stirring until totally combined.**

7 To the large mixing bowl, add half the dry-ingredient mix and half the milk. Stir, and then repeat with the remaining dry ingredients and milk, stirring until batter is silky smooth.

8 Divide that chocolaty goodness between the two cake pans. Bake it up for 30–35 minutes, rotating pans halfway.

FROSTING

1 cup heavy cream

2/3 cup granulated sugar

5 ounces dark chocolate chips

5 ounces semisweet chocolate chips

12 tablespoons butter, softened

1 In a midsized saucepan, stir the cream and sugar together over medium heat, until sugar is totally dissolved.

2 Reduce heat to low and add the chocolate chips. Stir until completely melted, and then remove saucepan from heat.

3 Using a hand blender, blend butter into that chocolate mixture, 4 tablespoons at a time, until smooth.

4 Cool frosting to room temp before using *(or suffer the consequences).*

So. Stinkin'. Good.

CRUNCH

1 box brownie mix

1/2 cup vegetable oil

1 Set oven to 300°F.

2 On a Silpat®-lined sheet pan, mix brownie mix with oil until fully combined and crumbly.

3 Bake 10–15 minutes until just set.

4 Cool completely.

TO ASSEMBLE:

1. Carefully remove devil's food cakes from cake pans and place on a clean surface.

2. Using an icing spatula or butter knife, spread a thin layer of chocolate frosting onto the tops of both cakes.

3. Pile brownie-streusel crunch on top of one frosted cake. Then place other cake, frosting-side down, on top of streusel layer.

4. Spread a thin layer of frosting over the entire cake, and then refrigerate until firm.

5. Once firm, spread final decorative layer of frosting over the entire cake, creating swirls or smoothing out as desired.

6. **To finish your devil's cake, decorate with sprinkles.** *(Gold disco dust on chocolate cake looks baller! But really, any sprinkle is a good sprinkle. And better than selling-out your soul to the devil, obvs.)*

LYIN' NO-GOOD CHEAT!

Ain't got time for that? Then simply frost the individual cakes with frosting & sprinkle with streusel. Yay!

HACK IT

A rubber spatula will do, but hands work the best. Get in there and make brownie-streusel magic!

STOP TEXTING ME, YOU CREPE

AKA:

OREO® CREPE CAKE

Truth: If friendships were emojis, they would all be Heart Eyes and Winky Faces and random 3 AM Kiss Marks — NOT Angry Faces and Middle Fingers and random 3AM Piles of Poo. So what are you waiting for? Stop that Thinking Face and Wavy Hand those Piles of Poo goodbye, once and for all.

CREPES

1/2 cup all-purpose flour

1 tablespoon unsweetened cocoa powder

2 tablespoon granulated sugar

1 egg

1 tablespoon unsalted butter, melted

1/2 cup milk

1. In a blender, dump in the flour, cocoa powder, sugar, egg, butter, and milk. Puree that stuff until all together and frothy.

2. Heat up a 10- to 12-inch nonstick skillet over medium-ish heat. Coat that baby with butter. Pour in 1/4 cup of the batter into the pan, swirl, coating the bottom of pan in a super-thin layer.

3. Cook until underside of crepe is goldenly delicious, about 2 minutes. Loosen and flip crepe, and then cook the other side for another minute or so. Set aside.

4. Keep it up until batter is gone, or you've got about 15 crepes.

WHIPPED CREAM

1 1/3 cups whipping cream, cold

1/4 cup granulated sugar

1 teaspoon vanilla extract

1. Dump whipping cream, sugar, and vanilla into a cold mixing bowl.

2. With an electric mixer, whisk ingredients on high until stiffened, about a minute.

OREO® CRUMBLES

7 Oreo® cookies, crushed

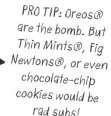

PRO TIP: Oreos® are the bomb. But Thin Mints®, Fig Newtons®, or even chocolate-chip cookies would be rad subs!

TO ASSEMBLE:

1. Place a single crepe on a large plate or serving platter or framed pic of your enemy.

2. Using an icing spatula or butter knife, spread a thin layer of whipped cream onto the crepe. Then sprinkle (KA-POW!) a small amount of Oreo® crumbles on top.

3. Layer up the crepes, whipped cream, and Oreo® crumbles until crepes are gonzo.

4. Top it off with the remaining whipped cream and Oreo® crumbles. And then more Oreo®. And then maybe a few more, etc. :)

EACH PERSON HAS MANY LAYERS. LIKE A CREPE CAKE OR AN ...

13

WHAT A PIECE OF
SHEET CAKE

Theirs. ↙

AKA:

CINCO LECHES CAKE
W/ MALTED MILK
WHIPPED CREAM &
DULCE DE LECHE
DRIZZLE

> Done right, leches
> cake is moist and
> fluffy — unlike your
> frenemy, who's just
> soggy and sad.

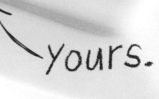

↖ **yours.**

CAKE

2 cups cake flour, plus extra for the pan

1 teaspoon baking powder

1 teaspoon salt

4 ounces butter, room temp

1 + 2 tablespoons granulated sugar

5 eggs

1 1/2 teaspoons vanilla extract

GLAZE

1 (12-ounce) can evaporated milk

1 (14-ounce) can sweetened condensed milk

1 cup half-and-half

TRUE LOVE IS LIKE EATING AN ENTIRE SHEET CAKE EVERYDAY. 98% IS GIDDY, SUGAR-HIGH HAPPINESS. BUT THERE'S STILL A BIG, OL' NUMBER 2% THAT'S NOT.

EAT MY WORDS

1 Crank up the oven to 350°F, and butter *(Yay!)* or spray *(Eh.)* a 13 x 9-inch baking pan.

2 Whisk together the cake flour, baking powder, and salt in a midsize bowl.

3 In a bigger mixing bowl, beat that butter on medium speed of a stand mixer *until it's learned its lesson* (or until fluffy), about a minute.

4 Drop the speed to low, and slooooooowly add the sugar during the next minute. Then stop and scrape down sides of bowl.

5 Crack in the eggs, one by one, mixing until each is totally combined.

6 Dump in the vanilla and mix to combine.

7 Add that flour mixture to the batter in three batches, mixing until just combined.

DO NOT OVER MIX!

8 Transfer batter to the prepared baking pan and spread evenly. (The amount of batter may appear pretty small, but don't worry!)

9 Bake for 20 minutes or until cake is all goldeny and scrumptious, turning halfway through cook time. Remove cake from oven.

10 Using a skewer or fork *(or shank)*, thoroughly stab that cake with small holes. Then set aside, allowing cake to bleed out — I mean, cool completely.

11 For glaze, whisk the evaporated milk, sweetened condensed milk, and half-and-half in a medium bowl until combined.

12 Pour glaze mixture over stabbed, cooled cake. Then wrap and refrigerate cake overnight.

HACK IT

If your electric mixer is an untrustworthy little prick, hand-mix that stuff.

WHIPPED CREAM

2 cups heavy cream

1 cup granulated sugar

1 teaspoon vanilla extract

3/4 cup vanilla malted milk

1 Dump the cream, sugar, vanilla, and malted milk into a cold mixing bowl.

2 With an electric mixer, whisk ingredients on high speed until fluffy, about a minute.

LYIN' NO-GOOD CHEAT!

*Ain't got time for that? Do this instead:
Buy a box of yellow or white cake, and follow the easy-to-follow instructions. Assemble with glaze from this recipe, 1 tub of Cool Whip® topping, and 1 squeeze bottle of dulce de leche topping.*

HACK IT

Longer or shorter cooking times could result in color/consistency variations. Experiment and find the dulce de leche that's muy bueno to you!

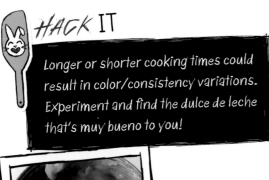

OKAY.

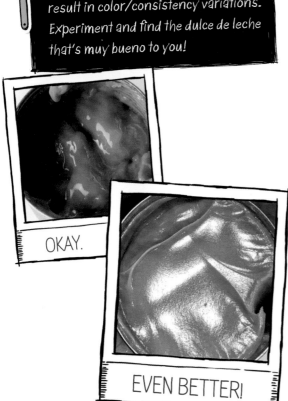

EVEN BETTER!

DULCE DE LECHE DRIZZLE

1 (14-ounce) can sweetened condensed milk

1 Peel the label from the unopened can of sweetened condensed milk, place in a medium saucepan, and cover completely with water.

2 Boil for 3-ish hours, replenishing water as needed to keep can fully submerged.

3 Remove from heat and cool the can to room temp.

4 Open can. *(Ta-da!)*

TO ASSEMBLE:

1. Using an icing spatula or butter knife, frost cinco leches cake with malted milk whipped cream. Top with fresh berries, if you're into that.

2. Drizzle dulce de leche on top, and then sprinkle with a pinch of salt. *(Any coarse salt will work!)*

HEARTS & FLOURS

ALL–PURPOSE FLOUR =
CARNATION

Perfect for just about any
occasion from sheet cakes to
funerals. (But not Valentine's
Day. Never.)

CAKE FLOUR =
ROSE

Like a rose, cake flour is perfect
for those tender moments
(i.e., tender cake, muffins, and
biscuits).

PASTRY FLOUR =
HONEYSUCKLE

Embrace this flour and you will
be amazed at what a little skill
and imagination can whip up.

Ok, consider this . . . You're totally into some dude/dudette. They're like your BFF, but you want to be more than just friends. So Valentine's Day rolls around, and a box of flowers arrives on your doorstep, inside your locker, or whatever, with a card that reads, "To: [Your Name Here] From: That Dude/Dudette." And you're, like, Oh man, this is it! You tear open the box to discover . . . yellow carnations. And then you're like, WTF. Because WTF.

Long story short, just like there's a flower for every occasion (i.e., I-just-wanna-stay-friends-so-here's-some-frickin'-yellow-carnations carnations), there's also a flour for every recipe. Check it.

BREAD FLOUR = DAISY

Bread flour and daisies are both simple & resilient — perfect for friendships or yeasty loafs on the rise.

WHOLE WHEAT FLOUR = MAGNOLIA

Robust and full of possibilities. Sometimes nutty or dense, but never too rough.

SELF-RISING FLOUR = FORGET-ME-NOT

Self-rising flour is not to be forgotten. Pre-mixed with baking powder and salt, it's perfect for biscuits and pancakes.

SHUT THAT STUPID *CAKE* HOLE

AKA:

COCONUT MOCHI CAKE W/ COCONUT SESAME–PECAN ICING

ZIP IT.

1 D Z.

60

Cut this rich, fully-fatted mochi cake into bite-sized* pieces.

*Actual "bite-size" may vary, depending on the size of your ex's or enemy's mouth. You know, like, normal sized. Or, a never-shuts-up-except-to-burp-up-week-old-backseat-chicken-nuggets-sized mouth.

CAKE

4 cups sweetened rice flour

1 tablespoon baking powder

3 cups granulated sugar

1/2 cup melted butter

4 eggs

1 (12-ounce) can coconut milk, full fat *(obvs)*

1 (12-ounce) can of evaporated milk, full fat *(double obvs)*

1 teaspoon vanilla extract

1/2 teaspoon almond extract

1 teaspoon coconut extract

1/2 teaspoon salt

1 Get the oven rolling to 350°F, and then butter up (or spray down) a 13 x 9-inch baking pan.

2 In a just-right bowl, stir together the rice flour, baking powder, and sugar.

3 In a big bowl, stir together all the remaining ingredients, and then add dry ingredients and mix until totally combined.

4 Pour this batter into the prepared baking dish, spreading evenly.

5 Bake about an hour or until center is golden and edges are all golden-brown.

ICING

2/3 cup of sugar

2/3 cup of evaporated milk

2 egg yolks

6 tablespoons butter

1/2 teaspoon vanilla extract

1/2 teaspoon salt

1 cup coconut flakes

1 cup of pecans, chopped

1/4 cup toasted sesame seeds

1 In a large-ish saucepan over low heat, whisk the sugar, evaporated milk, egg yolks, butter, and vanilla, until yolks thicken up. *DO NOT BOIL!*

2 Remove from heat and stir in the salt, coconut, pecans, and sesame seeds.

TO ASSEMBLE:

1 Using an icing spatula or butter knife or your tongue *(kidding-not-kidding)*, frost coconut mochi cake with coconut sesame pecan icing.

2 Slice that up and serve it warm.

#om

#nom

#nommmm

#burp

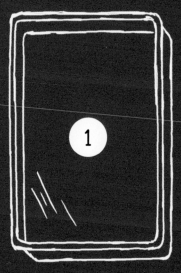

HALF SHEET PAN

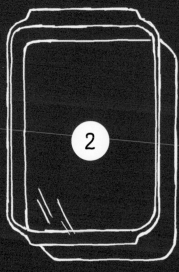

9 X 13 PAN

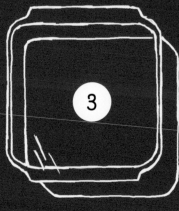

9 X 9 SQUARE PAN

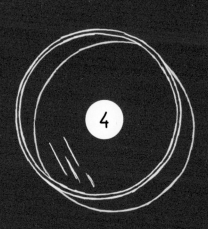

9 INCH ROUND CAKE PAN

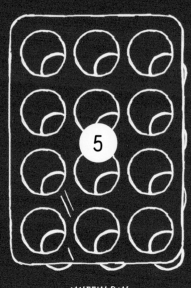

MUFFIN PAN

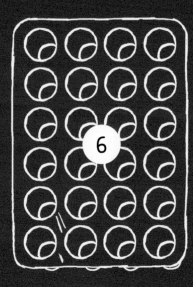

MINI MUFFIN PAN

9 X 5-INCH LOAF PAN

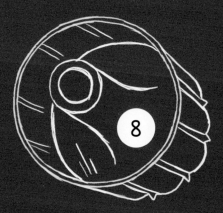

BUNDT PAN

PICK A *CAKE PAN* AND FIND OUT IF YOU'RE DATEABLE

1. You're a 100% stainless steel catch! Like a sheet pan, you're low maintenance and versatile. But you're also one smart cookie (not to mention smart toffees and brittles).

2. Anyone would be lucky to have you! Seriously! You might feel a bit average, but those other pans can't hold a candle to you (or a brownie or a cake . . .).

3. Don't let anyone call you square! From top to bottom, you're a must-have (especially for brownies, bars, and fudge).

4. You're complex — a pan of many layers, if you will. But if someone sticks with you, they're sure to end up in wedded bliss (or at least a three-layer wedding cake).

5. You're looking for someone who'll love every part of you (all twelve parts, that is). And believe me, there's someone out there with an appetite for that.

6. You like to micromanage, but don't let that hinder your dating game. Somewhere out there is a stud muffin who's just right for you!

7. Don't be afraid to raise you're expectations. . . .There are plenty of loafs out there, and you'd be a match made in leaven!

8. If you haven't heard, big Bundts are in! So drop that uniquely baked cake like it's hot (that's the best way to eat cake, after all).

15

THE ABSOLUTE CRUMB OF THE EARTH

AKA:

CRUMBY COFFEE CAKE

This coffee cake delivers one epic burn. You know, like, "Do you celebrate Earth Day . . .? No? Well, you should — because you're the crumb of it." Which is probably what you should've said instead of spending your breakupversary deleting all your S.O.'s pics from Instagram.

CAKE

1 1/2 cups all-purpose flour

1 cup granulated sugar

2 teaspoons baking powder

1/2 teaspoon baking soda

1/2 teaspoon salt

1 cup sour cream

1 teaspoon vanilla extract

2 eggs

STREUSEL

1 box cake mix *(your fave)*

1 teaspoon vanilla extract

1/3 cup oil

sprinkles, to taste → *(rainbow sprinkles, obvs!)*

1 Crank up the oven to 350°F, and prepare (butter or spray) a 9 x 9-inch baking pan.

2 In a big ol' bowl, mix together the streusel ingredients (cake mix, vanilla, oil, and sprinkles). Set aside.

3 In a medium-ish bowl, whisk together the flour, sugar, baking powder, baking soda, and salt.

4 In another bowl, beat the sour cream, vanilla, and eggs. Then add the dry cake ingredients and combine until moist. *(Again, ew!)*

5 Pour that batter into prepared baking dish, spreading evenly.

6 Then cover batter with crumby streusel and bake 40 minutes, or until center is set.

THERE ARE PLENTY OF

RAINBOW SPRINKLES
IN THE SEA.

SUCK IT UP AND GROW A *PEAR*

A pair-o-pears, fyi

AKA:

PEAR CHEESECAKE W/ GINGER GASTRIQUE

1 DZ.

60

Topping cheesecake with a pear is a bold move, imho. It takes confidence & courage & a whole lot of certainty. It takes — well, a big ol' pear, of course. But your ex or enemy probably liked their cheesecake w/ blueberries, amirite? Teeny-weeny, nearly nonexistent ones? Berries so tiny they looked like a couple of shriveled old raisins? It all makes sense now, doesn't it?

CHEESECAKE

**3/4 cups granulated sugar +
2 tablespoons for coating**

**16 ounces cream cheese,
room temp**

12 ounces chevre, room temp

1 tablespoon lemon juice

1 tablespoon vanilla extract

1/2 teaspoon salt

1 cup sour cream

6 eggs, room temperature*

**Note: If ingredients are NOT at
room temp, the mix will seize
and be lumpy.*

1. **Flip on oven to 350°F.**

2. **In a big mixing bowl, whip
   together the sugar, cream
   cheese, and chevre until
   silky and smooth. Then
   add remaining ingredients
   and mix until even silkier
   and smoother.**

3. **Pour the batter into a**
   9-inch springform pan.

4. **Bake in a water bath
   until completely set and
   slightly golden, about
   50–60 minutes.**

POACHED PEARS

1 quart water

1 1/3 cups granulated sugar

**4 pears, peeled, cored, and
quartered**

Optional:

Cinnamon stick

Whole cloves

Black peppercorns

Fresh lemon

Vanilla extract

Star anise

Fresh ginger slices

1. **In a large saucepan over
   medium heat, add the water
   and sugar, stirring until
   dissolved. Add optional
   ingredients, if you wanna.**

2. **Plop in the pears and
   simmer about 15–25
   minutes, or until pears can
   be sliced with a butter knife.**

3. **Remove those puppies from
   heat and let 'em cool in
   their liquid.**

GINGER GASTRIQUE

1/2 cup minced fresh ginger

6 ounces apple-cider vinegar

1 cup sugar

1. **In a small saucepan, bring
   the ginger and apple-cider
   vinegar to a boil.**

2. **Stir in the sugar, and then
   lower the heat and simmer
   for 20 minutes or so.**

3. **Strain and cool completely.**

GINGERSNAP SAND

8 ounces gingersnaps

2 tablespoons butter, melted

1/4 cup granulated sugar

2 teaspoons salt

1. **Using a food processor or
   your Wolverine claws, grind
   gingersnaps until crumbly.**

2. **In a medium-ish bowl, mix
   together the crumbled
   gingersnaps, butter, sugar,
   and salt, until fully integrated.**

CHEW ON THIS

The rim of a springform fastens to the
bottom of the pan w/ a clamp or spring,
allowing for easy removal of soft cakes
(i.e., perfect food porn pics!). However, if
looks aren't your thing (or you plan to eat
the cake directly out of the pan), a standard
9-inch round cake pan works A-OK.

TO ASSEMBLE:

1. **On a large plate or serving
   platter, layer gingersnap sand,
   cheesecake, and pears.**

2. **Drizzle with ginger gastrique.**

3. **Slice and serve it up!**

YOU'RE DRIVING ME
BANANAS

AKA:

ELVIS CUPCAKES

THANK YOU.
THANK YOU
VERY MUCH.

In the beginning, you said, I Can't Help Falling In Love. That Big Hunk O' Love is Always On My Mind. But he wouldn't commit, and you told him Love Me Tender — It's Now or Never, yo! For real! And Being A Fool Such as I, you believed him. But, that one Blue Christmas, he turned out to be a Devil In Disguise, a real Hound Dog, tbh, by ditching you One Night at the Heartbreak Hotel. (Thank you. Thank you very much. *curls lip*)

CUPCAKES

1 2/3 cups all-purpose flour

1/2 teaspoon salt

1 teaspoon baking soda

1/4 teaspoon baking powder

1 cup granulated sugar

1/3 cup butter, softened

2 eggs

3–4 medium bananas, ripened and mashed

1/3 cup water

1/2 teaspoon vanilla extract

1 **Crank up oven to 350°F. Then prepare (butter or spray) and line two muffin pans with cupcake papers.**

2 **In a midsize bowl, mix together the flour, salt, baking soda, and baking powder. Set aside.**

3 **In big bowl, mix together the sugar and butter until light and wonderfully fluffy. Then dump in the eggs, bananas, water, and vanilla, and combine.**

4 **Mix in the dry ingredients until just moistened.**

5 **Bake an hour, turning once.**

PEANUT BUTTERCREAM FROSTING

1/2 cup butter, softened

1 cup creamy peanut butter

3 tablespoons milk, or as needed

2 cups powdered sugar

1 **In a medium-ish mixing bowl, beat up that butter and peanut butter together with an electric mixer.**

2 **Slowly mix in the sugar. When mixture starts to thicken, add milk, one tablespoon at a time, until frosting is spreadable. About 3 minutes.**

BUTTERSCOTCH CANDIED BACON

1/2 pound bacon (or a pound, if you plan to NOMNOMNOMNOM)

8–10 hard butterscotch candies

1 Cook bacon until crispy, drain, and pat grease. Place cooked bacon on rimmed baking sheet, and set aside.

2 In a nonstick pan over low heat, CAREFULLY melt down butterscotch candies. Immediately pour over the bacon (Oh yeah!), spreading evenly.

3 Cool that stuff completely, and then break candied bacon into bite-sized pieces. *drools*

TO ASSEMBLE:

1. Using an icing spatula or butter knife, frost banana bread muffins with peanut buttercream frosting.
2. Top frosted muffins with butterscotch candied bacon.

(and then garnish with baby pickles, if you're feelin' crazy).

BACON LYFE.

DON'T TRY TO
BUTTER ME UP

AKA:

BUTTER POUND CAKE W/ SRIRACHA ICING

Truth: Dating is sometimes all about trusting your gut. Except if your gut's all HANGRY, ready to snap & gut-punch the next punk who gives it a stank eye. Only trust a gut that's hot-diggity happy on three pounds of pound cake. So eat up, k?

CAKE

2 1/3 cups all-purpose flour

1 1/2 teaspoon baking powder

1 teaspoon salt

1 3/4 cups granulated sugar

1 1/4 cups butter

2 large egg yolks

3 large eggs

2/3 cups heavy cream

1 1/2 teaspoons vanilla extract

Ingredients need to be at room temp!

1 Crank up oven to 350°F. Then butter up and flour-dust a Bundt cake mold.

2 In a medium-ish bowl, whisk all the dry ingredients together (flour, baking powder, and salt). Set that aside.

3 In a big bowl, whip the butter and sugar together until light goldeny and fluffy. Scrape down. Then add the eggs and yolks, one at a time, scraping down the bowl after each addition.

4 Dump in half of the dry mixture and half of the heavy cream. Mix. Scrape. Repeat.

5 Stir in vanilla until juuuuust combined. **DON'T OVERMIX** (you eager beaver, you).

6 Bake until a toothpick comes out cleanly from the center. About 30–45 minutes, depending on the size/shape of your Bundt mold.

ICING

1 8-ounce package cream cheese

1 stick butter

4 cups powdered sugar

Sriracha, to taste

1 Whip together the cream cheese and butter. Then slowly add powdered sugar until all's fluffy and delicious.

2 Squeeze in preferred amount of sriracha *(i.e., 1 tablespoon up to a crap-ton).*

TO ASSEMBLE:

1. Flip Bundt cake onto a serving platter, cut, and add a dollop of icing.

2. Or, take a bite of cake, a spoonful of icing, and assemble in your mouth.

RELATIONSHIPS AREN'T A PIECE OF CAKE. ONLY A PIECE OF CAKE IS A PIECE OF CAKE. THAT'S JUST REALITY.

EAT MY WORDS

19

NUTTY AS A FRUIT CAKE

AKA:

CRANBERRY-ORANGE PECAN CAKE

They say you can't judge a book by its cover. Well, fyi, you can't judge a dessert by its name. Because fruitcake. Unlike its namesake, this one is moist, tart, and actually-factually delicious. On the other hand, feel free to judge Chads, Trey's, Pams, and other nutjobs exclusively on their one-syllable names.

NUTJOBS

  2 DZ. 45

CAKE

1 1/4 cup granulated sugar

1 1/2 cups cranberries (fresh or dried)

2 teaspoons baking powder

1 1/2 cups all-purpose flour

1 cup powdered sugar

1/2 teaspoon salt

1/2 cup butter, melted

3 large eggs

1 orange, zested and juiced

1 teaspoon vanilla extract

1 cup sour cream

ME

A CHART OF DATING LYFE BY ME

1 Crank up oven to 350°F. Then butter up and flour-dust a Bundt cake mold.

2 Channel your inner fairy, and sprinkle 2 tablespoons of sugar and then 1/4 cup of the cranberries on the bottom of the pan. Set aside.

3 In a midsized bowl, whisk together the dry ingredients (baking powder, flour, salt, and sugar). Dump in the remaining cranberries.

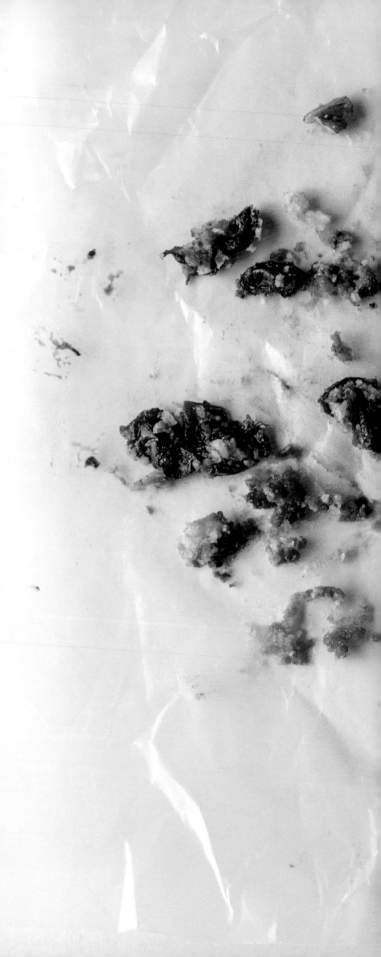

4 In a separate mixing bowl, cream together butter and sugar until pale-yellow and fluffy. Scrape down sides. Crack in eggs, one by one, and then mix until totally incorporated. Dump in orange juice & zest and vanilla and then sour cream.

5 Fold the dry ingredients into wet stuff and stir until just combined.

6 Pour this deliciousness in the prepared pan and bake 45 minutes (or until a toothpick comes out clean).

7 Pull the cake out of oven and allow to rest for 15 minutes *(POWER NAP!)*. Then flip cake onto a wire rack to cool.

GLAZE

1 1/4 cups powdered sugar

Pinch of salt

2 teaspoons lemon juice

1–2 tablespoons whole milk

1/4 cup dried cranberries, chopped

1/2 cup toasted pecans, chopped

Orange zest, to sprinkle

1 In a medium-ish bowl, dump in the powdered sugar, salt, juice, and milk until totally combined.

2 Drizzle the glaze over cooled cake and then sprinkle with cranberries, pecans, and orange zest.

THE
BEST
THINGS
IN LIFE
MAKE YOU
SWEATY.

I NEVER KNEADED YOU ANYWAY

BREADS & PASTRIES

20

DON'T CALL ME HONEY BUNS

AKA:

CINNAMON ROLLS W/ HONEY GLAZE

Ever split a big, brunch-worthy cinna-roll w/ someone, and they eat the entire ooey-gooey center and leave you the crusty edges? (A total crime against pastry!) You don't need that type of self-centered person in your life. Seriously! Gift them a batch of these bad boys, and tell 'em, "Eat your freakin' heart out!" They don't know what they're missing.

  2 D Z. 10

OOEY-GOOEY CENTERS OF ATTENTION

ROLLS

2 teaspoons active dry yeast

1 cup whole milk, warmed to 110°F

1/2 cup granulated sugar

1/4 cup butter, softened

1 teaspoon salt

2 eggs

4 cups all-purpose flour

FILLING

1 cup brown sugar, packed

2 tablespoons cinnamon

1/3 cup butter

1 In a big ol' bowl, dissolve the yeast in that cozily warmed milk. Then mix in the sugar, butter, salt, eggs, and flour until totally combined.

2 Suffocate that bowl in plastic wrap, set in a warm place, and let dough to rise for an hour or until doubled in size. *(Watch it grow!)*

3 Meanwhile, in a medium-ish mixing bowl, combine all the filling ingredients and set aside.

4 Crank up oven to 400°F.

5 On a floured surface, roll out the dough into a rectangle, approximately 1/4-inch thick.

6 Using an icing spatula or butter knife *(or your middle finger)*, spread the cinnamon-roll filling across the dough evenly.

7 Roll dough lengthwise into a long, cylinder shape. Then cut that dough into 2-inch slices and place into the greased-up pie pan, spacing at least 1 1/2 inches apart.

8 Bake that deliciousness 10 minutes or until lightly golden-brown.

GLAZE

1 1/2 cups powdered sugar

3 1/2 tablespoons water

2 tablespoons honey

Pinch of salt

1 In a small bowl, mix all ingredients to desired thickness. *Easy-peasy!*

TO ASSEMBLE

1. Slo-mo drizzle half of that honey glaze over cinnamon rolls while still hot.

2. Reserve remaining half of honey glaze, and drizzle atop individual rolls immediately prior to serving. *Mmm . . .*

TEXT MESSAGE BREAKUP

Peanut Butter & Jelly (aka PB&J)

Jelly
You still turn my legs to jelly

PB
Aww... You're so sweet

But...

This isn't working

Jelly
WHAT?! WHY?!

PB
I'm just spread too thin at the moment, babe

and tbh you're just not my jam

Jelly
but you said we'd always stick together

PB
Yeah well...

I'm nuts

OMG

THE TWO OF US ARE *TOAST*

ME + YOU=

AKA:

MILK BREAD ROLLS & NEXT–DAY GRIDDLE TOAST

These soft, buttery, OMG–did–Thanksgiving–come–early–this–year bread rolls are one thing you won't regret tomorrow (because Next-Day Griddle Toast!). Just be sure they're not the ONLY thing!

MILK BREAD ROLLS

1/2 cup granulated sugar

1 tablespoon active dry yeast

2 tablespoons butter

2 cups whole milk

2 teaspoon salt

5 cups all-purpose flour

1 In a large mixing bowl, combine sugar, yeast, and butter.

2 In a small saucepan, warm over medium-low milk to 110°F. Immediately pour over dry-ingredient mixture. Wait 5 minutes.

(ticktock ticktock)

3 Add salt and 4 1/2 cups flour, and then mix with bread hook for 8 minutes.

4 Cover bowl with plastic wrap and set in a warm place. Allow dough to rise approximately an hour or until doubled in size.

5 Pour dough onto surface covered with 1/4 cup flour and divide into twelve equal pieces.

6 Roll each divided piece of dough into a smooth ball and place onto a parchment- or Silpat®-lined baking sheet, 2 inches apart.

7 Spray dough balls with nonstick cooking spray or brush with melted butter, and then cover with plastic wrap for 30 minutes.

8 Preheat oven at 350°F.

9 Bake aboiut 20 minutes, turning halfway through the bake time. Bread is done when centers are golden and bottoms are golden-brown.

10 Serve hot!

NEXT−DAY GRIDDLE TOAST

day-old milk bread rolls

butter, softened

salt

granulated sugar

1 Slice day-old milk bread rolls in half and generously butter both sides.

2 Sprinkle lightly with salt and/or sugar.

3 In a skillet over medium-high heat, cook butter rolls until golden brown.

THE *YEAST* OF YOUR WORRIES

Did you know yeast is alive? Like — L.I.V.I.N. — livin'? Seriously! This tiny organism munches on the starches in flour, producing carbon dioxide (we all get a little gassy sometimes, amirite?) and making dough expand and rise. But hey, you say! I can't even nurture a GD relationship. I'll kill those little microbes in a microsecond. To that I say, NAY! On a list of things to worry about, yeast should be, well, the least or your worries. But here are a few tips to raise (<<< see what I did there?) your spirits:

№1: NOT MY TYPE

Instant, active dry, rapid, fresh cakes . . . ? WTF! When it comes to yeast, there's a lot of different types. Luckily, they all work interchangeably (kinda like swapping out the groom at a wedding). Active dry is stable and easy to use, so why not put a ring on that thing and stick w/ it!

№2: I'VE GOT PROOF!

"Proofing" yeast — or proving your yeast is alive — is the biggest scam in the yeast-scamming world. There, I said it. To proof active dry yeast, dissolve in warm water, according to instructions. But pro tip: don't do this! If your ADY is fresh, it's alive. Just spoon it directly into your recipes.

№: RAISING HECK

I got one word for you: "Allow-your-dough-to-rise." Watch it double in size — like your confidence after dumping that loser ex or enemy — and you'll be all good, OK?

22

WHAT A TOTAL D—
BAGEL

AKA:

CHOCOLATE—BAGEL PUDDING W/ CREAM CHEESE ICE CREAM

Dating is like a baker's dozen of day-old bagels. Sometimes you pull out a poppy seed or a good-old reliable plain. But tbh, more often than not, it's a pumpernickel or GD cinnamon-raisin, and you wind up with a food-baby or — best-case scenario — sticky fingers. Don't give up, people. . . . Your everything is out there.

NOT
v
I'M WITH STUPID

PUDDING

1 pound plain bagels *(preferably day-old)*

1 cup heavy cream

1 cup granulated sugar

1/4 cocoa powder

1/2 teaspoon salt

6 ounces semisweet chocolate chips

6 ounces dark chocolate chips

2 large eggs

2 large egg yolks

2 cups whole milk

1 tablespoon vanilla extract

1 teaspoon chocolate extract

HACK IT

Water Bath How-To: Place your baking dish or muffin pan into a larger pan or rimmed baking sheet. Fill the outside pan with a small amount (a fingertip worth) of hot water, and then pop in the oven. Voilà!

1 Chop up bagels into small, dice-sized cubes (about 7 cups).

2 In a large stockpot, stir the heavy cream, sugar, cocoa powder, and salt until boiling.

3 Remove that stuff from heat and immediately add the semisweet and dark chocolate chips. Let that stand for a couple minutes, and then whisk until smooth.

4 In a midsized bowl, whisk together eggs, yolk, milk, and extracts. Mix this combo into the chocolate, and then stir in bagel cubies, combining.

5 Suffocate that mixture with plastic wrap, making sure the bread is completely covered in liquid. Fridge it for a couple hours or overnight.

6 Get the oven rolling to 325°F.

7 Pour chocolate-bagel pudding mixture into a buttered-up 8 x 8-inch baking dish. → *(or large muffin pans for bite me-sized servings).*

8 Bake that goodness in a water bath *(see HACK IT, above!)* until completely set and slightly golden and center feels firm, about an hour for an 8 x 8-inch dish or 35 minutes for muffins.

9 Let cool to remove, but serve it up warm.

ICE CREAM

1 1/2 cups heavy cream

1 (8-ounce) package cream cheese, room temp

1 (14-ounce) can sweetened condensed milk

3/4 cup cherry pie filling *(or fave flavor)*

1 packet (or 1 heaping teaspoon) instant coffee

1/2 cup graham crackers, crushed *(or fave cookies)*

1 In a large-ish mixing bowl, whip heavy cream until stiff peaks form. Scrape into another bowl and set aside.

2 In the dirty mixing bowl *(Yay! No dishes!)*, beat up that cream cheese until smooth. Then add sweetened condensed milk and beat again *(TKO!)* until smooth.

3 Fold whipped cream into cream-cheese mixture, careful not to deflate whipped cream.

4 Pour half of the cream mixture into a plastic-wrapped, 9 x 5-inch loaf pan. Then drizzle with half of the cherry pie filling, and sprinkle on half of the instant coffee and crushed graham crackers. Swirl that awesomeness with a spoon or finger or whatever.

5 Dump on the remaining cream mixture, and top with the rest of the cherry pie filling, instant coffee, and crushed graham crackers. Swirl that stuff again.

6 Cover with plastic wrap and freeze until firm, about 4 hours or so.

7 Serve it up warm with chocolate the bagel pudding!

DONUT
CALL ME
AGAIN

AKA:

MOCHI DONUTS W/ LEMON—NUTMEG GLAZE & COFFEE DIP

Has someone left a hole in you? Then serve up this Sweet Revenge and let them know you're still one frickin' sweet, sexy & delicious donut!

STARTER DOUGH

1/4 cup glutinous rice flour

3 tablespoons of whole milk

DONUTS

1 3/4 cups sweet rice flour

1/2 cup whole milk

2 1/2 tablespoons unsalted butter, melted

1/4 cup granulated sugar

1 egg

1 teaspoon baking powder

4 cups neutral-tasting oil, for frying

GLAZE

2 1/2 tablespoons unsalted butter, melted

1 cup powdered sugar

1/2 teaspoon vanilla extract

1/2 teaspoon lemon peel, grated

Nutmeg, to taste (freshly grated, if possible)

2–3 tablespoons hot water

1 Mix starter dough ingredients together in a microwave-proof bowl, and nuke that stuff for 30 seconds. Then set aside to cool for 5 minutes or so.

2 Meanwhile, in a large stand mixer bowl, mix donut ingredients (not the oil) with a dough hook. Dump in starter dough and continue mixing until totally combined.

3 Dust a clean surface with rice flour and roll out that dough to 1/2-inch thick. Using a donut cutter (or two concentric cutters), cut as many donuts *as your broken heart desires.*

4 Okay, time to make the donuts! Heat oil in a big pot over medium heat until it reaches 350°F on a candy thermometer. Drop in a few donuts and watch them sink and then float back up. *(You can't keep a good donut down!)* Fry for a few minutes on each side until golden & fluffy & delicious looking. Transfer donuts to a paper towel-lined tray to drain that nasty grease.

5 For glaze, mix the butter, powdered sugar, vanilla, lemon, and nutmeg in a small bowl. Dilute that stuff with 2–3 tablespoons of hot water to desired consistency *(i.e., runny or thick AF).*

6 To assemble, dip one side of each donut into glaze.

COFFEE DIP

1 cup sweetened condensed milk

1/3 cup espresso (or strong instant coffee)

1/4 teaspoon almond extract

1/2 teaspoon vanilla extract

1/2 teaspoon salt

Bittersweet memories *(optional)*

1 Dump all ingredients into a small bowl and whisk until combined or until bittersweet memories *(optional)* are fully disintegrated.

2 This Sweet Revenge is best served warm.

CHEW ON THIS

Glutinous rice flour is also called sweet rice flour. Ironically, this flour is neither glutenous nor sweet. (LIARS!!) It is, however, RICE — a starchy, sticky-wicky rice that can thicken and bind like no other. (Scout's honor!)

LUBE UP

(AKA KNOW YOUR OILS)

Before things get all hot & heavy, make sure you have the right kind of oils on hand (and wherever else you need it *wink wink*). But with hundreds of options, choosing the right one can be a, er, slippery slope. A few things to consider:

№ 1: OH-SO-TASTY

Like some relationships, some oils can leave a bad taste in your mouth. For real. Coconut & olive oil might be perfect on a salad, but they'll leave your dessert tasting like, well, coconut & olive oil. Neutral-tasting oils, like vegetable, canola, and even corn oil, won't.

№ 2: YOU'RE SMOKIN'

Oils with the highest smoke point — basically, the temp the oil begins to smoke — is an important factor in baking/cooking. High smoke point oils, like canola, vegetable, sunflower, peanut, and sunflower, won't leave you burned.

№ 3: COST

Look, I can make it rain with the best of them (dolla bills, y'all!), but you don't need to spend those Benjamins on oil. You just don't. Choose a good, responsibly sourced oil, and you'll be smooth sailing.

BITE ME, SCUM *MUFFIN*

BITE ME.

AKA:

FIVE–SPICE DONUT MUFFINS W/ COCONUT DIP

Love conquers all? REALLY?! Whoever said that (probably someone on a horse) never ate a muffin. Like, excuse me, sir, but muffins conquer all. For real. If love & muffins went to war, muffins would storm the love-wall, kill all the love-people, and plant their muffin-shaped flag atop the love-castle. Yay, muffins!

3 DZ.

20

MUFFINS

3 cups all-purpose flour

1 tablespoon baking powder

1 teaspoon salt

1/2 teaspoon ground nutmeg

1/2 teaspoon cinnamon

1 cup granulated sugar

4 tablespoons butter, softened

2 large eggs

1/2 teaspoon vanilla extract

1 cup whole milk

1 Kick things off by cranking the oven to 350°F. Then butter up a couple 12-cup muffin pans.

2 Dump the flour, baking powder, salt, nutmeg, and cinnamon into a large bowl and stir.

3 In another bowl, cream together the sugar and butter. Add the eggs and vanilla and mix again.

4 Add the flour mixture and milk alternately to the creamed mixture, beating well and scraping the sides of bowl down after each addition.

5 Fill the prepared muffin pans about 2/3 full. Bake until golden, 15–20 minutes or so.

IF THEY CAN'T TAKE THE HEAT, GET THEM OUT OF YOUR KITCHEN. CUZ IT'S YOURS.

EAT MY WORDS

DIP

3 large egg yolks

1/2 cup + 2 tablespoons granulated sugar

1/4 teaspoon salt

1 tablespoon cornstarch

1 cup coconut milk

1 teaspoon pandan extract

1 In a medium-ish saucepan, whisk together the yolks, sugar, salt, and cornstarch until smooth.

2 Pour in coconut milk and bring this mixture to a boil, whisking constantly. In a couple-o-minutes, when mixture thickens to pudding, take off heat.

3 Stir in extract and let that custardy deliciousness cool for a bit.

CHEW ON THIS

WTF is pandan extract? Glad you asked! Also known as pandan essence or screw pine paste (yes, really), this natural flavoring/colorant comes from the palm-like leaves of the pandan plant, which is found in southeast Asia and the Hawaiian islands. Often used to flavor jasmine rice, pandan has a nutty, vanilla-like flavor. You can find this extract at Asian market, but vanilla extract would be a B-team substitute.

CHEW ON THIS

Haven't heard of five spice? Then LISTEN UP! This blend of five spices (um . . . duh) is often used in Vietnamese or Chinese cooking. In fact, it's sometimes called Chinese five spice (thank you, Captain Obvious). Yeah, yeah, just tell me the five spices, you say? Clove, cinnamon, fennel, star anise, and Szechuan pepper. There.

TOPPING

1 cup sugar

1 tablespoon five spice

1 tablespoon cocoa powder

1 stick butter, melted

1 Mix the sugar, five spice, and cocoa in a small bowl.

2 Coat muffins in melted butter, and then immediately roll them in mixture.

3 Transfer to a cooling rack or serve 'em up fresh AF.

NOT MY CUP OF *TEA*

AKA:

BLACK TEA SHORTBREAD

For some, the aroma of coffee and/or tea brings back memories of budding relationships: flirty-flushy midnight rendezvous, sweaty palms, caramel-latte-flavored kisses, and comfortable lovey-dovey silences. For others, it doesn't. Here's some shortbread.

2 sticks butter, room temp

1/2 cup powdered sugar

2 teaspoons finely ground black tea

2 cups all-purpose flour

1 teaspoon vanilla extract

Pinch of salt

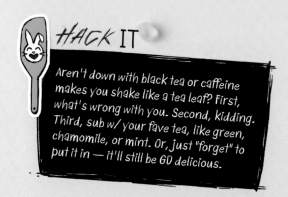

HACK IT

Aren't down with black tea or caffeine makes you shake like a tea leaf? First, what's wrong with you. Second, kidding. Third, sub w/ your fave tea, like green, chamomile, or mint. Or, just "forget" to put it in — it'll still be GD delicious.

1 Crank oven to 350°F, and then line a cookie sheet with a Silpat® or parchment paper.

2 In a large mixing bowl, cream the butter and sugar together until pale-golden and fluffy and *oh-so delicious.*

3 Dump in the tea, flour, and vanilla and mix until everything's together and harmonious, *like a budding relationship.*

4 Dust a clean surface with powdered sugar. *(No, this isn't a typo! Powdered sugar NOT flour!)* Gently roll out dough to 1/2-inch thick and cut into desired shapes. (Cute middle fingers would work, just sayin'.)

5 Bake 10–12 minutes or until just golden.

NOT MINE

YOU

MIXING

BEAT

To create a smooth creamy mixture by stirring briskly, using a spoon, whisk, or mixer. Hands, elbows, feet, or the nearest object are also allowed.

CREAM

To enthusiastically beat the daylights out of your ingredients, usually your sugar or a fatty food. Result: fluffy smoothness. And a sense of peace.

GRIND

To utterly mortify, diminish, and pulverize any food by crushing it into teeny, tiny bits. Once you've finished it, no one will ever mess with your kitchen again.

MARTIAL ARTS

POUND

To thump or strike repeatedly, with great force. Also a unit of weight or a sweet, rich cake made from equal parts flour, sugar, butter, and rage.

WHIP

To add air and/or volume with a whisk or mixer or leather flogger. Sizes of tool may vary.

ZEST

1. The outer, colorful rind or peel of a citrus fruit. 2. The exhilaration you feel after performing all the mentioned activities.

26

THEY DIDN'T CUT THE MUSTARD

THE CHEESE

AKA:

CORNBREAD W/ HONEY-MUSTARD BUTTER

> *Things Your Ex Could Cut:*
> The Cheese
> A Muffin
> One Loose
> A Fart
>
> *Things They Couldn't Cut:*
> The Mustard

CORNBREAD

1 cup cornmeal

3 cups all-purpose flour

1 1/3 cups granulated sugar

2 tablespoons baking powder

1 teaspoon salt

2/3 cup vegetable oil

1/3 cup melted butter

2 tablespoons honey

4 eggs, beaten

2 1/2 cups whole milk

HONEY–MUSTARD BUTTER

1 stick butter, room temp

1 tablespoon honey

1 teaspoon dry mustard

1/2 teaspoon of salt

1 **Flip on oven to 350°F. Then butter up a 9 x 13-inch baking dish and set aside.**

2 **In a large mixing bowl, whisk together the dry ingredients (cornmeal, flour, sugar, baking powder, and salt).**

3 **Dump in the oil, butter, honey, eggs, and milk, and stir just till moist.**

4 **Pour that** *moist-moist-moisety-moist* **batter into the prepared baking dish and bake for about 45 minutes, or until a toothpick comes out cleanly and cornbread is golden-brown and** *cracklicious.*

5 **Meanwhile, plop the honey-mustard butter stuff into a food processor and pulse** *(unst unst unst!)* **until combined.**

6 **Serve cornbread hot out of the oven — with butter melting on top, obvs.**

MYOB
(MIND YOUR OWN *BISCUITS*)

27

AKA:

STRAWBERRY BISCUITS
W/ CHICKEN–SKIN CANDY

Yeah, yeah, so your last friendship was oh-so good. Like, good-good. Chicken-and-waffles good. But now your waffle is gone (or maybe your chicken?), and you're like, "boo-hoo" no more chicken and waffles. *sheds single tear* STOP! Replace that soggy ex-Eggo w/ a fresh, super-hot biscuit. K? You're welcome.

1 DZ.   15

BISCUITS

2 cups all-purpose flour

2 teaspoon salt

1 tablespoon baking powder

1 tablespoon granulated sugar

1 1/2 cups heavy cream

Sugar, for sprinkling

1 Crank oven to 425°F, and then line a cookie sheet with Silpat® or parchment paper.

2 In a large bowl, mix all dry ingredients (flour, salt, baking powder, and sugar). Then add cream, and — guess what? — mix again!

3 Using an ice-cream scoop or a large cookie scoop, plop mounds of dough onto the prepped sheet. Then flatten those little suckers with your palm to about 1-inch thick. Sprinkle with sugar, if desired.

4 Bake for about 15 minutes or until golden.

Serve
HOT-HOT-HOT!

JAM

1 cup strawberries, pureed

1 cup granulated sugar

1/4 cup apple-cider vinegar

1 teaspoon pectin, powdered

1 cup strawberries, diced

Salt & black pepper, to taste

1 In a medium-ish saucepan, heat 1 cup of pureed strawberries, 1/2 cup of the sugar, and the vinegar until hot.

2 Stir in the powdered pectin and another 1/2 cup of sugar. While whisking, heat to boil, then simmer for about 3 minutes. Remove from heat.

3 When cooled to room temp, dump in diced strawberries and salt & black pepper. Whisk together. Refrigerate till needed *and before you eat the whole GD bowl.*

WTF DOES IT MEAN?

Not all acronyms are created equal. In baking, qt isn't your "cutie," and a # isn't a hashtag. So check out this list below. IMHO, it'll increase your baking IQ X 10.

Tbsp = tablespoon

Tsp = teaspoon

C = cup

lb = pound

= pound

mL = milliliter

kg = kilogram

pt = pint

qt = quart

oz = ounce

g = gram

gal = gallon

°C = degrees Celsius

°F = degrees Fahrenheit

hr = hour

min = minute

doz = dozen

pk = peck

dash = > 1/8 teaspoon

pinch = > 1/8 teaspoon

ICING

2 cups powdered sugar

1 tablespoons butter, softened

1/2 teaspoon salt

1/2 teaspoon vanilla extract

1/2 cup maple syrup

1 In a just-right bowl, stir all that stuff together until spreadable. Easy-peasy!

CHICKEN–SKIN CANDY

1/2 pound chicken skin (about 3-thighs worth)

Granulated sugar

Kosher salt

Freshly ground pepper, to taste

1 Crank up oven to 350°F. Trim excess fat from chicken skin and then cut into 3-inch pieces.

2 Dredge skin in sugar, and then season with salt & pepper.

3 Flatten, flesh-side down, on a parchment paper-lined baking sheet. Top with another sheet of parchment and baking sheet (to keep skin from curling).

4 Bake until browned and crispy and *WTF-is-this-gloriousness enlightenment*, **about an hour.**

5 Remove top baking sheet and paper and let cool 10 minutes.

TO ASSEMBLE:

1. **Split hot biscuits!**

2. **Scoop strawberry filling onto a biscuit, and serve with a dollop of maple icing and chicken-skin candy.** *Heck yeah!*

HACK IT

When baking chicken skin candy, be careful not to burn the sugars. It should look like this:

Not this.

Or this.

HACK IT

PRO TIP: Bake skin-candy ahead of time and store it in an airtight (and skin-burglar proof) container in the fridge for 1–2 days.

SUCH A COLD—
TARTED BASTARD

AKA:

CHOCOLATE–
PRETZEL TART
W/ EARL GREY
WHIPPED
CREAM

PIES VS. TARTS VS. FRENEMIES

PIES	TARTS	FRENEMIES
Top crusts and/or crusty toppings	No tops	Nothing up top
High sides	Shallow sides	Shallow all over
Delicious fillings	Delicious fillings	Dead inside

CRUST

3/4 cup butter

3 tablespoons granulated sugar

2 1/2 cups crushed pretzels

1 **Mix all that stuff together and then press firmly into a greased tart pan.** *(You could do that blindfolded, I bet!)*

GANACHE

6 ounces heavy cream

1 packet (or teaspoon) instant coffee

12 ounces semisweet chocolate chips

3 tablespoons corn syrup

Pinch of salt

1 teaspoon vanilla extract

1 **In a medium-ish saucepan, warm heavy cream and coffee over low heat until steaming.**

DO NOT BOIL.
(Seriously, yo!)

2 **Remove cream from heat, add chocolate chips, and wait a couple minutes.** *(tick tick tick . . .)* **Then stir until smooth.**

3 **Dump in the corn syrup, salt, and vanilla and stir again.**

4 **Pour this mixture into your mouth — I mean, into the prepared pretzel-tart crust and fridge it for about 4 hours (preferably, overnight).**

5 **Serve cold,** *like your frenemy's heart.*

WHIPPED CREAM

1 tablespoon Earl Grey tea leaves

(about 2 packets of tea)

1 cup heavy cream

2 teaspoons sugar

1 **In a small bowl, stir Earl Grey tea leaves into the heavy cream. Then cover and refrigerate this mix for 8–12 hours.** *(NO LONGER!)*

2 **Strain the cream into a medium bowl, pressing on the tea leaves to extract as much liquid as possible. Discard the tea leaves.**

3 **Whip the heavy cream with the sugar, or fridge it and whip up to a day later.**

CHEW ON THIS

Who the heck is Earl Grey? He was, in fact, a real dude — the UK's prime minister from 1830–1834, to be exact. He somehow got a black tea flavored with bergamot named after him. Although I doubt he ever lifted a pinky finger to actually make his own tea, ya know. Typical.

BAD FRIENDSHIPS ARE LIKE CHOCOLATE.

THEY MELT DOWN QUICKLY.

WORLD'S GREATEST POS (PIECE OF *STRUDEL*)

AKA:

STREUSEL STRUDEL

The WORLD'S GREATEST = the best, the cannot-be-topped, the absolute, honest-to-goodness perfect thing in the world. This POS is THAT. Your ex and/or enemy? The opposite of that.

STREUSEL

1/3 cup granulated sugar

2 tablespoons all-purpose flour

2 tablespoons butter

1/2 teaspoon cinnamon

Pinch of nutmeg (fresh, if possible)

1 Mix all ingredients with your *(preferably clean)* hands until crumbly. That's it!

HACK IT

Fyi, people that name things (I assume they work for the Naming Things Foundation) are total liars! Like, you'd assume nutmeg is a nut, amirite? WRONG. It's a seed. A seed from a GD EVERGREEN TREE. So write to your reps at the NTF and ask them, "WTF?" (And, side note: People w/ nut allergies are totally fine consuming this not-a-nut nut. Yay!)

STRUDEL

1/2 17.3-package puff-pastry sheets, thawed

3 ounces cream cheese, softened

1/4 teaspoon cardamom or cinnamon

4 ounces bitter chocolate, chopped

1 Flick on the oven to 400°F.

2 Unfold the pastry sheets on a lightly floured surface. Cut sheet in half to form two rectangles. Fold one rectangle in half the long way.

3 Using a big, sharp, *"this-is-a-knife"* knife, cut nine slits through the folded side to within 1/2 inch of the opposite edge.

4 In a small bowl, stir together cream cheese and cardamom/cinnamon.

5 Spread mixture to within half an inch of the pastry edge. Sprinkle with chocolate, and then sprinkle with half of the streusel.

6 Unfold the pastry and place it over the edge, and then press edges to seal.

7 Sprinkle remaining half of the streusel on top of the pastry.

8 Bake for 15 minutes or until golden brown and puffily perfect.

WORLD'S GREATEST POS VOTING BALLOT

Choose a winner (loser?) — it's your civic duty!

[ ] SERIAL KILLERS

[ ] OIL TYCOONS

[ ] BULLIES

[ ] LIARS

[ ] PEOPLE WHO HATE CATS

[ ] PEOPLE WHO HATE CHOCOLATE

[ ] PEOPLE WHO COME BACK TO HAUNT YOU AFTER THEY'RE DEAD

[ ] PEOPLE WHO DON'T COME BACK TO HAUNT YOU AFTER THEY'RE DEAD

[ ] YOUR EXES & ENEMIES

Only one can be the WORLD'S Greatest!

PLEASE *TURNOVER* A NEW LEAF

AKA:

RHUBARB TURNOVERS W/ RHUBARB COMPOTE & RHUBARB GASTRIQUE

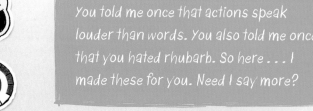

You told me once that actions speak louder than words. You also told me once that you hated rhubarb. So here . . . I made these for you. Need I say more?

144

COMPOTE

4 cups rhubarb, diced

1 cup sugar

Pinch of salt

1 **In a small saucepan, stir rhubarb and sugar together. Let sit for about 10 minutes or until water leaches out of fruit.**

2 **Cook on low for another 15 minutes, keeping fruit bright and textured** *(not brown and soggy and sad).*

3 **Drain fruit into containers — reserving liquid for gastrique** *(see below).*

RHUBARB GASTRIQUE

4 parts rhubarb-liquid: 2 parts sugar : 1 part apple cider vinegar

1 **In a small saucepan, warm gently on low until sugar is completely dissolved.**

TURNOVER

1 package puff pastry, cut into squares

1 egg, whisked

Sugar in the raw, for sprinkling

TO ASSEMBLE/BAKE:

1 **Heat oven to 350°F.**

2 **Place puff pastry square on a Silpat®- or parchment-lined baking sheet.**

3 **Plop some rhubarb compote into the center of each square.**

4 **Fold squares over into a triangles, and then seal the edges by crimping w/ a fork or pinching like teeny-tiny pies**

5 **Lightly brush the entire top of the turnover with whisked egg. Sprinkle with a butt-load of sugar.**

6 **Bake until puffy, flaky, and golden-browny. Serve up this Sweet Revenge w/ a drizzle of gastrique.**

YUMMA IN MA TUMMA!

 CHEW ON THIS

Don't let the name fool you. Gastrique is not as complicated as it sounds (nor as yucky!). It's simply a fancy-schmancy word for a reduction of sugar and vinegar (aka sweet-and-sour deliciousness). So take a stabby-stab at it.

IT'S NOT YOU, IT'S BRIE

AKA:

BAKED APPLE BRIE CROUTE

Most friendships & relationships aren't 100% sweet & light & golden like a perfectly puffed pastry. But they shouldn't always be moldy, pungent bricks-o-cheese either. Like this dessert, a stinky-sweet combo is key to I-couldn't-eat-another-bite, unbutton-your-pants fulfillment.

1 pound Brie (wheel or wedge)

1 puff-pastry sheet, thawed

1 egg yolk

Apple slices

1 Get that oven rollin' to 400°F and line a sheet pan with parchment paper.

2 Unfold puff pastry and wrap around Brie — folding, stretching, kicking, punching, and smoothing, until cheese is totally covered.

3 Slap Brie, seam-side down, on the parchment-papered pan. Then brush egg yolk over the entire dome.

4 Bake for 30 minutes or until golden-brown. Then let stand for about 45 minutes. *(Or the entire thing will leak out all weird and oily and disgustingly!)*

5 Eat warm with tart apples.

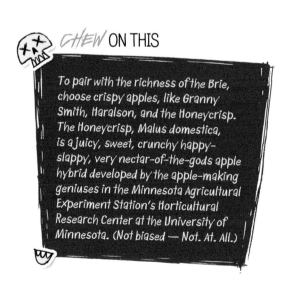

CHEW ON THIS

To pair with the richness of the Brie, choose crispy apples, like Granny Smith, Haralson, and the Honeycrisp. The Honeycrisp, *Malus domestica*, is a juicy, sweet, crunchy happy-slappy, very nectar-of-the-gods apple hybrid developed by the apple-making geniuses in the Minnesota Agricultural Experiment Station's Horticultural Research Center at the University of Minnesota. *(Not biased — Not. At. All.)*

BUH-BYE, SWEET STUFF

CANDIES, CREAMS & MORE

GO *FUDGE* YOURSELF

31

AKA:

MACKINAC ISLAND CHOCOLATE FUDGE W/ WHITE CHOCOLATE CANDIED RAMEN

Don't let anyone tell you the way to someone's heart is through their stomach. Because, fyi, it's not. To do that, you'd want to make a vertical incision just above the breastbone, and then crack the sternum to open the chest cavity and reveal the heart. And if anyone says otherwise, tell them to go fudge themselves. You're smarter than that.

FUDGE

4 cups granulated sugar

1 cup milk

1 cup butter, room temp

25 large marshmallows

2 cups (12 ounces) milk chocolate chips

2 cups (12 ounces) semisweet chocolate chips

2 ounces unsweetened chocolate, chopped

1 teaspoon vanilla extract

1 **Butter up (or spray) a foil-lined 9 x 13-inch baking pan. Set aside.**

2 **In a large saucepan, dump in the sugar, milk, and butter and combine. Boil that stuff over medium-ish heat, stirring constantly.** *(You can do it!)* **Once boiling, cook for a couple minutes without stirring and then remove from heat.**

3 **Stir in marshmallows until melted. Stir in chocolate until melted. Then add vanilla extract and stir** *(Keep it up!)* **until all ingredients are totally combined.**

4 **Immediately pour into prepared baking pan, spreading evenly.**

5 **Cool at room temp for an hour or so, and then top with the candied ramen.** 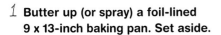 *(See next page . . .)*

6 **Cover and fridge it for 3 hours or until firm.**

7 **Using foil, lift out fudge and cut into bite me-sized pieces.**

CANDIED RAMEN

1 package instant ramen noodles
(Seasoning packet discarded or devoured)

1 cup white chocolate chips

2 tablespoon butter

1 teaspoon salt

1 **Crank up the oven to 350°F. Boil them oh-so delicious ramen noodles according to the package directions. Then rinse under cold water and drain ramen dry.**

2 **Next, prepare a rimmed baking sheet with nonstick cooking spray, and then spread ramen onto the sheet.**

3 **Bake for 30–40 minutes, turning sheet every 15 minutes for even baking, until ramen is golden-brown and crispyily RAMAZING. Remove from oven and cool.**

4 **In a small saucepan, melt together white chocolate chips and butter over medium heat, stirring constantly.** *(Feel the burn!)*

5 **Drizzle melted mixture over cooled ramen, and then sprinkle with salt.**

6 **Cool candied ramen at room temp for about an hour.**

7 **Using a meat tenderizer** *(aka a smashy-smasher)***, break candied ramen into small pieces and set aside.**

HACK IT

PRO TIP: Uncooked instant ramen is a Grade-A after-school/after-work snack. Crush the noodles inside the pack, open & sprinkle on the seasoning, shake the bag, & enjoy! P.S. You're welcome.

BAKING IS THERAPY. TRUST ME — FUDGE NEVER GETS TIRED OF LISTENING TO YOUR PROBLEMS.

EAT MY WORDS

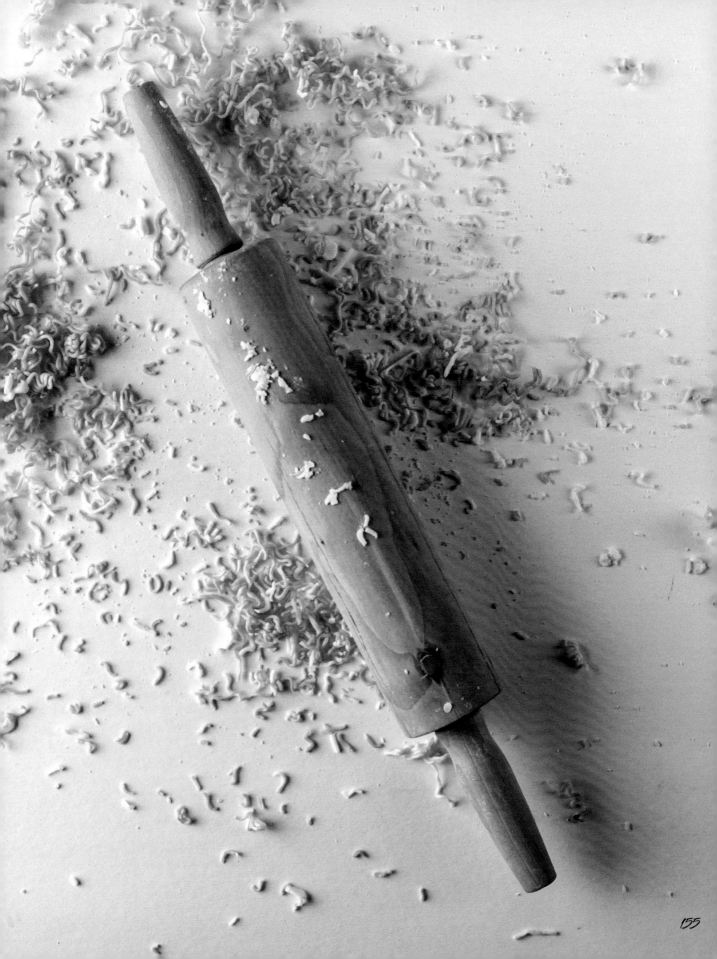

32

WHAT AN ABSOLUTE *NUT* JOB

AKA:

CRACKER JACKS® NUT BRITTLE

15

Everyone's heard the old clichés comparing relationship progress to baseball, right? You know, like, how a kiss equals making it to first base. And, like, how when someone heads for second base, you get bored and start looking for the peanut vendor ("Peanuts! Get yer peanuts here!"), and by third base you're knee-deep in shells. And then everyone's suddenly cheering, and you're like "Hellz yeah, I ate that whole bag!" No . . . ? Never? Huh.

1 cup butter

1 cup granulated sugar

1 cup brown sugar

1 cup corn syrup

1 teaspoon vanilla extract

1/2 teaspoon baking soda

1 pound peanuts, dry-roasted and salted

1 box Cracker Jacks®

HACK IT

Ain't got Cracker Jacks®? No problem! (Well, except for the fact that you're missing out on rockin' those in-the-box temporary tattoos!) Replace w/ caramel corn or hard cereals, like Cap'n Crunch®, Kix®, or some fall-festive Apple Jacks®.

1 Preheat oven to 250°F, and get a sheet pan prepped w/ Silpat® or parchment paper.

2 In a medium saucepan, boil the butter, sugars, and corn syrup for 5 minutes.

3 Take off heat and stir in the vanilla and baking soda. Then stir in the peanuts. *(Do not over-stir, you greedy bastard)*

4 Spread this scrumptiousness out onto the prepped sheet and cook for 45 minutes, stirring every 15 minutes or so.

5 Remove the sheet from the oven and immediately stir in Cracker Jacks®.

6 Cool completely and then — *WHAM-O!* — smash into pieces with a mallet or a five-fingered octagon *(i.e. yo fist).*

HOW TO SPOT A NUT

Dating is like a bunch of nuts — a total mixed bag. But if you're planning to partake, you should at least be able to identify one nut from the other. So here's your visual nut guide:

THE ALMOND

THE CASHEW

THE MACADAMIA

THE WALNUT

THE PECAN

WHEN YOU SEE ONE

33

WHAT A BUNCH OF SOUR GRAPES

AKA:

SOUR–GRAPE PANNA COTTA

Ever see one of those Renaissance paintings of some naked chick kickin' back while a loincloth-wearing dude feeds her grapes. And you're thinking #GOALS, amirite? Well, I bet those grapes were sour AF.

0

SOUR GRAPE GELATIN

**1 teaspoon unflavored gelatin
(from a 1/4-ounce envelope)**

1 cup grape juice

1 tablespoon lemon juice (preferably fresh)

**1 cup red and/or green seedless grapes,
thinly sliced**

PANNA COTTA

1 envelope unflavored gelatin (about 1 tablespoon)

2 tablespoons cold water

2 cups heavy cream

1 cup half-and-half

1/3 cup sugar

1 1/2 teaspoons vanilla extract

1 In a small-ish saucepan, sprinkle the gelatin
over 1/4 cup grape juice until softened, about
5 minutes or so.

2 Bring gelatin to a simmer, stirring until
dissolved. Remove from the flame and stir
in the remaining 3/4 cup grape juice, lemon
juice, and grape slices.

3 **Prepare six ramekins** *(see Hack It below)* **w/
nonstick cooking oil. Divide the grape-licious
mixture among ramekins and freeze until set,
about 30 minutes.**

4 **Meanwhile, bloom more gelatin in a small
saucepan over water. Stir additional gelatin
mixture over low heat until dissolved.
Set aside.**

5 **In a large saucepan, stir the cream,
half-and-half, and sugar to a boil. Then
remove pan from heat and stir in gelatin
mixture and vanilla. Strain.**

6 **Divide cream mixture among prepped
ramekins and chill, covered, at least 4 hours
or overnight.**

TO SERVE:

**Dip ramekins, one at a time, into a bowl of hot
water for about 3 seconds. Run a thin knife
around edge of each ramekin and flip onto a
serving dish.** *(Or, run your tongue around edge of each
ramekin and flip into mouth!)*

HACK IT

Ramekins are small, ceramic bowls,
perfect for baking individual desserts. For
this recipe, if you don't have ramekins
(and you rame-CAN'T), a silicone muffin
tray or an ice tray would work in a pinch.

34

I AIN'T *PUDDING* UP WITH THIS

AKA:

BUTTERSCOTCH PUDDING POTS W/ CHOCOLATE SAUCE

They say love is patient. Well, this recipe takes a little patience as well. But you're probably better off waiting on a pudding pot than a soul mate or a BFF. Unless, of course, a pudding pot is your soul mate or BFF. Then WINNING!

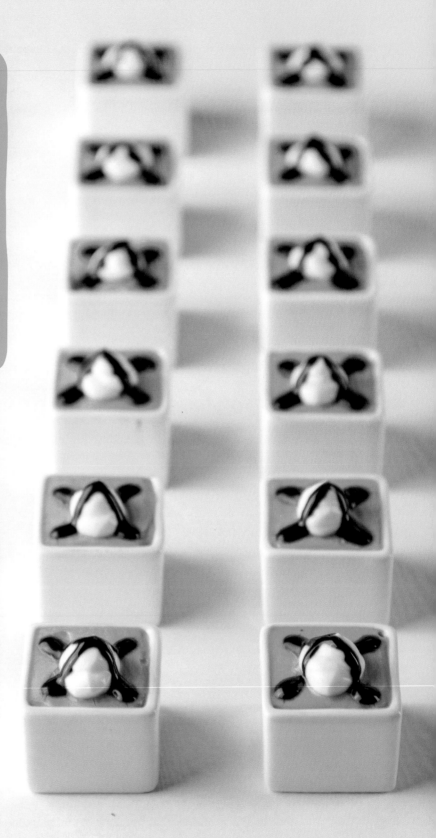

BUTTERSCOTCH POT DE CRÈME

4 tablespoons butter

1 cup brown sugar, packed

4 cups heavy cream

1 teaspoons vanilla extract

1/2 teaspoon salt

8 large egg yolks

Sour cream

Butterfinger®, crushed (optional)

1 **Dump butter and sugar into a midsized saucepan and stir together over medium heat. Cook until this mixture starts to brown and smoke ever so slightly, or about 15–20 minutes.**

2 *Slo0Ooo0owly* **add the cream, a cup at a time. Cook butterscotch until any crystalized sugar dissolves again. Then add the rest of the cream, vanilla, and salt.**

(Oh my!)

3 **Next, whisk those yolks — and do not stop! Add some of the hot butterscotch cream while continuing to whisk. Once the yolks are warm to the touch, dump the yolks into the pot of hot butterscotch and gently whisk.**

4 **Strain the mixture, and then crank the oven to 325°F.**

5 **Divide the custard into the ramekins. Then place the ramekins in a water bath (fyi, water should be hot!) and loosely tent with foil.**

6 **Bake for 25–40 minutes, or until the pudding pots** *jiggle like a bowl full of jelly.*

7 **Finally, remove the pan from oven and cool completely. Fridge it for at least an hour — unless you like room-temp pudding, ya weirdo.**

CHOCOLATE SAUCE

2 ounces dark-chocolate chips

3 tablespoons heavy cream

Pinch of salt

1 **In a small saucepan, stir all ingredients together over low heat. Easy-peasy!**

TO ASSEMBLE

Plop a spoonful of sour cream into each pudding pot, drizzle-whizzle with chocolate sauce, and sprinkle with crushed Butterfinger®, if desired.

CHEW ON THIS

A totally random and not-at-all-related-to-pudding fact: The servings icon used throughout this book is modeled after Fortune Cat, known in Japan as Maneki Neko. In Japan and China this cat (page 81 & 198), often seen waving or beckoning in restaurants and store windows, is thought to bring good luck. And GOOD LUCK sharing these servings with your exes & enemies and not eating them all by your unlucky-in-love self.

35

ROTTEN TO THE *COEUR*

AKA:

COEUR A LA CRÈME

In French, coeur a la crème means "heart with cream," since traditionally the dessert is molded into a heart shape. Quite possibly the perfect gift for that enemy or ex who's traditionally heartless.

HACK IT

Cheesecloth is a thin, meshy cloth available at kitchen supply stores, hardware stores, etc. Ain't got time for that? No worries! Coffee to the rescue (per usual)! Replace the cheesecloth w/ large coffee filters or paper towels or panty hose or torn bedsheets. What the what? Yep.

4 10 x 10-inch squares cheesecloth

1 (8-ounce) package cream cheese, room temp

1 cup sour cream

6 tablespoons powdered sugar, divided

1 teaspoon lemon juice (preferably fresh)

1/2 teaspoon vanilla extract

Pinch of salt

2 cups fresh fruit (Your fave!)

1 Dampen the cheesecloth with water and line four molds with a square of cheesecloth each.

2 In a large mixing bowl, whip the cream cheese, sour cream, 4 tablespoons powdered sugar, lemon juice, vanilla, and salt in large bowl until smooth, about 4 minutes.

3 Strain this deliciousness and divide among the molds. Then fold cheesecloth over and cover with plastic wrap.

4 Chill completely (at least a couple of hours, but overnight is fine too).

TO ASSEMBLE

1. Unwrap the molds and flip them onto plates.

2. Top with your fave fresh fruit and sprinkle with powdered sugar, obvs.

1

2

5

6

3

4

7

8

36

YOU *DIM SUM,* YOU LOSE SOME

AKA:

EGGY CUSTARD DIM SUM

Still thirsting over a former S.O.? Don't sweat it. Seriously, DON'T. Because the only thing worse than cyberstalking your ex is cyberstalking your ex while you have a bad case of B.O.

YOU SUCK.

CRUST

1 package puff pastry dough

1 egg, beaten

FILLING

1/2 cup granulated sugar

1/2 teaspoon cornstarch

1/2 teaspoon salt

3/4 cup whole milk

2/3 cup heavy cream

8 large yolks

1 teaspoon vanilla extract

1 Heat oven to 375°F. Lightly grease/ butter up a 12-cup muffin tin.

2 Cut puff pastry into squares, pressing them firmly into the muffin tin.

3 Dump the sugar, cornstarch, and salt into a medium bowl and whisk. Then add in milk, cream, yolks, and vanilla and whisk again until combined.

4 Fill each cup with custard to about 1/8-inch from the top of the crust. Brush edges with egg wash. Bake until crust is golden and custard is just set, about 20 minutes.

5 Cool in the pan for 15 minutes and then move to a wire rack to cool completely.

LIKE, FOR REAL

CHEW ON THIS

WTF is dim sum? Put simply it's a traditional Chinese food served in small portions & shared. Although it can be anything really (tiny bites of chicken, pork, etc.) dumplings served in steamer baskets are dim sum faves!

37

A HOT MESS

AKA:
ETON MESS

> What's the difference between a hot mess and a cold mess? One is your former S.O. wearing an ironic T-shirt and cargo shorts, and the other is them wearing a snowsuit. Otherwise, same.

4 cups fresh strawberries

2 cups whipping cream

2 teaspoons sugar

1/2 teaspoon vanilla extract

Pinch of salt

1 package meringues
(If you're gutsy, see below . . .)

HACK IT

If you're using subpar strawberries, or berries out of season, add a little fresh lemon juice and sugar until deliciousness ensues.

1 Chop up the berries. Set aside.

2 Using an electric mixer, whip the cream and sugar on high speed until fluffy and peaking.

3 Stir in vanilla and salt until totally combined.

TO ASSEMBLE:

1. Top meringues with whipped cream and strawberries, alternating layers. That's it!

— — — — — — — — — —

MAKE YOUR OWN MERINGUES, YO!

1 1/2 tablespoons cornstarch

1 1/2 cup granulated sugar

6 egg whites (about 1 1/2 cups)

1/3 teaspoon cream of tartar

Pinch of salt

1 1/2 teaspoons vanilla extract

1 Ready, set, GO! Crank up oven to 275°F and line a sheet pan with parchment paper or Silpat®. *(You know the drill by now.)*

2 In a tiny bowl, whisk the cornstarch and sugar. Set aside.

3 In large mixing bowl, whip the egg whites, cream of tartar, and salt on medium for about 2–3 minutes or until a rabid-white froth forms. *(GRRRRR . . .)*

4 Mix in the cornstarch and sugar and whip until fluffy. When stiff glossy peaks form, add the vanilla extract.

A Hot Mess mess?

5 With a large spoon, plop little bird nest-like shapes onto the prepped sheet pan.

6 Bake for about 20–30 minutes and turn. Repeat until meringues are dry and bottoms are pale yellow.

38

WHEN I THINK OF US,
ICE CREAM

AKA:

FLAMIN' HOT CHEETOS® ICE CREAM SANDWICHES W/ FLAMIN' HOT CHEETOS® GANACHE

15

Truth bomb: Every person's gonna have something that annoys you. Just be sure the good outweighs the bad. Like Cheetos®, for example. They kickbutt, right? But, at the same time, presenting a class project w/ fluorescent-red fingers kinda sucks. But still Cheetos®. Good > Bad.

FLAMIN' HOT CHEETOS® SUGAR

Granulated sugar

1 bag Flamin' Hot Cheetos®, ground

1 Mix sugar to Flamin' Hot Cheetos® at a ratio of 2:1.

SUGAR COOKIES

2 cups all-purpose flour

1 cup Flamin' Hot Cheetos®, ground

2 teaspoons baking powder

1/2 cup butter

1 cup granulated sugar

2 eggs

1 Crank up oven 350°F.

2 In a medium bowl, mix the flour, Flamin' Hot Cheetos®, and baking powder. Set aside.

3 In a separate bowl, cream the butter and sugar until pale-yellow and fluffy. Add eggs, one by one, until totally combined. Then dump in the dry ingredients and combine.

4 Scoop dough into large ball and roll into Flamin' Hot Cheetos® sugar. Then press them balls onto a parchment- or Silpat®-lined baking sheet until cookies are about 1/2-inch thick.

5 Bake for about 15 minutes, turning halfway through baking time. Cookies are done when fluorescent red (Epic!) and medium-soft to the touch.

GANACHE

2 ounces Flamin' Hot Cheetos®, food processed into fine crumbs

1 cup heavy cream

1 cup white chocolate chips

1 In a medium saucepan set over medium-high heat, stir Flamin' Hot Cheetos® into heavy cream. Bring the liquid to a boil, then remove the pan from the heat.

2 Mix and melt white chocolate in. Set aside to cool.

TO ASSEMBLE:

1. Choose 2 cookies of similar shape and size. Place cookie face down on a plate.

2. Scoop ice cream on top of cookie, spoon ganache over ice cream, and top with second cookie.

DESSERTS &
RELATIONSHIPS
NEED THE
RIGHT AMOUNT
OF SPICE.
OTHERWISE . . .

39

WE'RE DEAD & BERRIED

AKA:

BERRY PALETAS

Fool me once, shame on you. Fool me twice, make popsicles. Seriously! These sweet, berrylicious pops will make all your troubles melt away. Not really, but they're still OMG-good.

4 cups fresh berries *(Your faves!)*

1 cup granulated sugar

1/2 cup orange juice

Pinch of salt

2 tablespoons lemon juice

1 Stir berries and sugar together in a medium saucepan and rest for 15 minutes or so. Add orange juice and salt.

2 Bring everything to a boil, reduce heat, and simmer for 5 minutes. Then remove from flame and cool to room temp.

3 Pour *fruity funsies* into a blender and lemon juice. Blend.

4 Divide between popsicle molds, cover with the lid, and add in the Popsicle sticks.

5 Freeze for about 5 hours, or until completely frozen.

CHEW ON THIS

Paletas are ice lollies made with fresh fruit, popularized in street food culture and originating from Mexico and Central America.

HACK IT

No Popsicle molds? DIY! First find a food safe small container (tiny disposable cups, large ice-cube mold, etc.) and cut a piece of sturdy construction paper or cardboard to fit over it. Poke a hole in the center of it large enough for a Popsicle stick and voila! Popsicle lyfe.

40

I'M NOT FONDUE YOU

AKA:

HOT CHOCOLATE FONDUE

This ooey-gooey chocolate fondue-y is nearly 100% perfect. Still, it's missing something. . . . A dipstick. But you shouldn't have any trouble finding one of those, amirite? Or maybe two? Or three . . . ?

CAUTION:
CONTAINS
BITTERSWEET
MEMORIES

1 cup semisweet chocolate chips

2 tablespoons butter

1 (14-ounce) can sweetened condensed milk

2 tablespoons coffee

Pinch of salt

1 teaspoon vanilla extract

1 In medium-ish saucepan, melt down the chocolate, butter, milk, and coffee. Cook and stir constantly until thickened, about 5 minutes. Remove from heat. Add salt and vanilla.

2 Serve warm as a fruit and cookie/cracker dipping sauce or drizzle over ice cream or cake. *(Or just eff it all and eat by the GD spoonful.)*

I HATE YOU A *LATTE*

AKA:

LATTE TOBLERONE® SEMIFREDDO

For this fancy-schmancy, semi-frozen dessert any chocolate will do. So feel free to substitute — it's totally replaceable. You know, like your last S.O. or BFF.

SEMIFREDDO

3 tablespoons instant coffee

4 large eggs, separated

1 tablespoon vanilla extract

1/4 cup granulated sugar

4 ounces Toblerone® or other Swiss chocolate, finely chopped

1 1/4 cups heavy cream

1. Cover a loaf pan in plastic wrap and line up three medium bowls.

2. In bowl #1, dissolve the instant coffee with egg yolks, vanilla, and sugar.

3. In bowl #2, beat the egg whites until stiff.

4. Without cleaning the whisk *(Yay! No dishes!)*, beat bowl #1 until thick.

5. Still not cleaning the whisk *(WHAAA—?)*, beat cream until it holds its shape. (If you beat everything in order, you don't need to wash the whisks in between. Score!)

6. Fold the cream into the coffee mixture, then carefully fold in the whites. Fold through the Toblerone® and tip into the loaf tin. Lightly cover the surface with plastic wrap. When frozen, overwrap in foil and freeze.

7. To serve, unwrap and turn onto a platter, popping semifreddo out by pulling at plastic wrap. Top with chocolate coffee beans and chopped chocolate.

CHOCOLATE COFFEE BEANS

2/3 cup semisweet chocolate chips

1 1/2 teaspoons vegetable shortening

1/2 cup coffee beans

1. In a small bowl, nuke chocolate chips and shortening until melty and smooth.

2. Dip the coffee beans in chocolate and allow excess to drip off.

3. Place each bean on waxed paper and let stand for 10–15 minutes or until firm.

4. Serve w/ latte and get amped!

CHEW ON THIS
Don't be intimidated by semifreddo! Semifreddo is just fancy Italian for a semi-frozen dessert. A semi-dessert is perfect for that semi-frenemy.

HORO*SCOOPS*

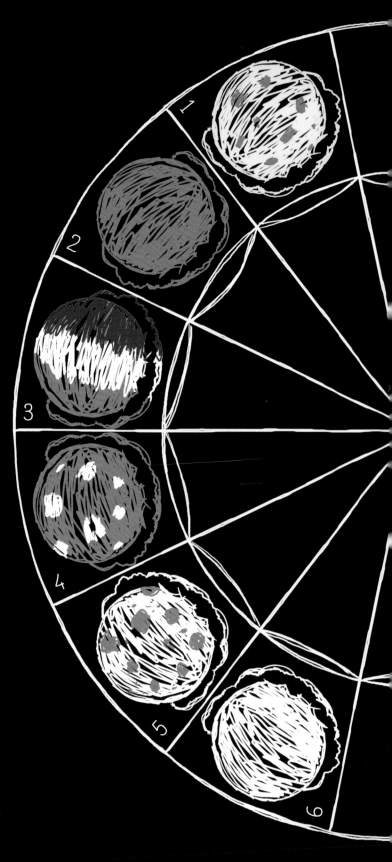

1. BUTTER PECAN
(March 21–April 19)

You're a daredevil — some might even call you a bit of a nut. But you're also whip-smart & buttery smooth. Find someone who'll enjoy the rich complexity of you.

2. CHOCOLATE
(April 20–May 20)

Your personality ranges from semisweet to decadently dark. Everyone wants a piece of you. Just make sure you save a percentage of yourself (85% cacao?) for yourself.

3. NEOPOLITAN
(May 21–June 20)

You're complex, self-reliant, and multidimensional (3D, to be exact). Your carton doesn't have room for any more flavors right now, tbh, and you couldn't be happier. Three cheers to that, "STRAWBERRY! VANILLA! CHOCOLATE!"

4. ROCKY ROAD
(June 21–July 22)

Admit it — sometimes you get a little nuts (we all do!), which is why a lot of your relationships are, well, rocky. If you want to cool things off, though, it's time to mallow out. If not, then stay on the same path — er, rocky road.

5. COOKIE DOUGH
(July 23–August 22)

You're an ooey-gooey, sugary sweet, surprise-in-every-bite type of person. One taste and anyone would be hooked. Which is why you're hesitant to share. Because more for them = less of you.

6. VANILLA
(August 23–September 22)

You're not one to brag, but you're perfectly fine on your own! Practical, consistent, and pretty dang tasty, if you don't say so yourself (which you won't). That'll make it all the more unexpected when you find your perfect pair. The chocolate to your vanilla, if you will.

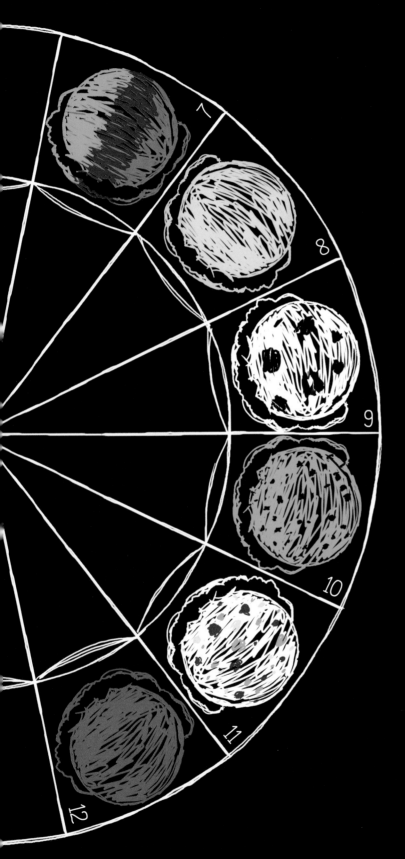

7. SPUMONI
(September 23–October 22)
Your worldly & romantic & satisfying — the punctuation mark to a great Italian feast, if you will. When you finally find true love (which you will), well, that's amore!

8. SALTED CARAMEL
(October 23–November 21)
You'll soon meet the nougat to your caramel. You'll let them experience the sweet, sticky side of you. But a minor difference ("It's pronounced "KAR-muhl!!") will bring out your salty side.

9. COOKIES & CREAM
(November 22–December 21)
You like to have fun — even get a little crazy sometimes. But inside that kooky exterior is a soft & sweet center that no one could resist.

10. MINT CHOCOLATE CHIP
(December 22–January 19)
Your ambitions get in the way of developing long-lasting friendships. In fact, others often think you have a chip on your shoulder. But don't let that deter you! Those who take the time to know you will discover that chip is pure, mint-chocolate confidence.

11. TUTTI FRUTTI
(January 20–February 18)
When people meet you, they don't quite know what to expect. They ask are you fruity? Are you tutti? (And WTF is a tutti anyway?) The answer: Everything they've been missing.

12. ORANGE SHERBET
(February 19–March 20)
You're a total wild card — a dreamy creamsicle of imagination. Heck, you're not even ice cream! Some people will like that. Some people won't. Orange you glad you don't give AF?

42

SUCH A *PIZZA* CRAP!

Personal pan pizza (i.e. NOT anyone else's)

AKA:
DESSERT PIZZA

Pizza toppings should be a deal breaker. Never — I mean, never-ever compromise. You want bacon, peanut butter, and bananas on your 'za? Or maybe sardines, sausage, and onions (ya weirdo)? Go on & GET IT. Order that stuff w/ an ETA of 30 minutes or less. Don't let anyone convince you otherwise. Cuz, fyi, a cheese pizza ain't worth the GD delivery fee.

SNICKERDOODLE CRUST

2 3/4 cups all-purpose flour

2 teaspoons baking powder

1 teaspoon salt

1/2 cup of butter

1 cup granulated sugar

2 eggs

1 **Crank up the oven 350°F**

2 **Line a pizza pan with parchment paper and grease w/ nonstick cook spray.**

3 **Mix the flour, baking powder, and salt in a medium bowl. Set aside.**

4 **In a separate bowl, cream the butter and sugar until pale yellow and fluffy. Then crack in the eggs, one by one, until totally combined.**

5 **Combine dry and wet ingredients.**

6 **Press cookie dough into a large, round pizza shape, until approximately 1/2 inch thick.**

7 **Sprinkle with sugar. And also sprinkles, if desired.** *(All the sprinkles!)*

8 **Bake for 20 minutes, turning halfway through baking time. Cookie is done when pale yellow and firm to touch in the center.**

9 **Cool completely.**

FROSTING

10 ounces white chocolate chips

1 cup sour cream

1/2 teaspoon vanilla extract

Pinch of salt

1 In a medium saucepan over low-low heat, melt white chocolate chips, stirring often.

2 When creamy and completely melted, take off heat and stir in the sour cream and vanilla.

BUTTERSCOTCH FUNYUNS®

12 hard caramel candies

1 medium gas station-sized bag of Funyuns®

1 cup butterscotch chips

2 tablespoons butter

1 Food processor blitz or beat the hard caramel candies into tiny chips and dust. Set aside.

2 Lay out Funyuns® in a single layer on a cookie sheet.

3 Melt butterscotch and butter in microwave, at 15-second intervals.

4 Dip Funyuns face down into butterscotch and then immediately into candy dust.

5 Yum!

TO ASSEMBLE:

1. Place butterscotch Funyuns® atop the pizza.

2. Slice and serve.

HACK IT

Don't limit yourself to Butterscotch Funyuns! Get creative. Get crazy, even, and top this pizza with whatever the frick you want. Seriously, hit up the gas station snack aisle and challenge yourself & your tastebuds? Want to top this Pizza Crap w/ Skittles? Why not! Want beef jerky on your 'za? Go right ahead! Donut? Don't mind if I do! The choice is up to you (and the inventory of your local gas station).

LIKE SWEET & SALTY, OPPOSITES ATTRACT . . .

EXCEPT WHEN THEY DON'T.

FRUCK OFF!

AKA:

PEANUT CORN–CHIP CANDY

Sometimes opposites attract. Like corn chips & candy, sweet & sour, peanut butter & pickles (for real!). But when they don't, you can either force-swallow and fake-smile your way through it. Or, you can spit it into a napkin, feed it to alley cats, and never make the same mistake again. Your choice.

10 1/2 ounces Fritos®

1 cup salted roasted peanuts

1 cup granulated sugar

1 cup light corn syrup

1 cup creamy peanut butter

1 cup Reese's Pieces® Candy

1 Dump corn chips and peanuts onto a greased or Silpat®-lined 10 x 15-inch sheet pan.

2 Next, bring the sugar and corn syrup to boil. Then remove from heat and stir in peanut butter until smooth.

3 Pour that mixture evenly over chips and nuts. And then evenly sprinkle candy over it all.

4 Cool to room temp and smash into pieces.

CHEW ON THIS

I'm not just being crass (per usual) — Fruckies is an actual thing. (Look it up, y'all!) It's a sweet-salty brittle/crackle with Fritos. But for the life of me I can't find the origin of this word. Let's assume the "Fr" in Fruckies stands for Fritos. Then WTF does the "uck" stand for? Can't be "yuck," right — cuz these are GD delicious. Seriously, if you know, give me call. Or, better yet, just text me.

WITH SYMPATHY
FOR YOUR LOSS
(OF *ME*).

HAPPY
BREAKUPAVERSARY!

BE MY
EX–VALENTINE

I HOPE THIS IS
AWKWARD FOR YOU.

ROSES ARE RED,
VIOLETS ARE BLUE,
EAT ME.

JUST BECAUSE . . .
YOU SUCK.

THINKING OF YOU
*(GETTING STUNG
BY A BEE)*

GIMME SOME SUGAR.
*(COOKIES
AREN'T CHEAP.)*

#BLESSED
#BECAUSEINEVER–
HAVETOSEEYOU*AGAIN*

KEEP THE *PAN.*

CONGRATS ON YOUR
DOUCHINESS!

FOR YOUR GRADUATION
(. . .TO *SINGLE LIFE*).

TO: _____

FROM: _____

TO: _____

FROM: _____

TO: _____

FROM: _____

TO: _____

FROM: _____

TO: _____

FROM: _____

TO: _____

FROM: _____

TO: _____

FROM: _____

TO: _____

FROM: _____

TO: _____

FROM: _____

TO: _____

FROM: _____

TO: _____

FROM: _____

TO: _____

FROM: _____

ACKNOWLEDGMENTS

I am only able to do what I love because of the unfathomable support and generous hearts of these freakishly brilliant, beautiful, and amazing people:

My editor, Donald Lemke, and Bob Lentz, Karon Dubke, Sarah Schuette, and the entire SWEET REVENGE team at Capstone — I am so incredibly grateful to you for giving me this opportunity and transforming my recipes into the cookbook of my dreams.

My Hola Arepa family, especially Christina Nguyen, whose unwavering friendship and dynamic support in my eccentric baking is the whole reason I'm the pastry chef that I am.

My MPLS Tattoo fam, who loved, supported, and featlessly ate my entire test-kitchened cookbook, including the weirder edits that didn't make it.

Kate Macleod Kim, my ride or die.

The incorrigible Scott Leben, love of my life, owner №1 to Maximus & Nietzsche, eater of my fries. Thanks, dude, for supporting me through portrait painting, maxillofacial prosthetic delirium, becoming a pastry chef, my tattoo artist career, and now writing this book. What's next? Just kidding. (Kind of.)

There's been a whole lot of dramatic loss & unbelievable luck throughout this past year. I'd like to give a grateful shout-out to my unbelievably supportive family & friends: Yoomi An Larmee, Meghan Shinduk Kim, Lochin Smith, Lana Bosak, Taylor Dobson, Bree Ann Rapp, Sarah Shin Thorpe, Miriam Raya, Kyle Wolford, Dana Hathaitham, & Elina Camarena Bascom.

Although I know they will hate to be mentioned, I am eternally grateful to Matt Schmidt and Sun Cowles, whose fault it is that I became a cook in the first place.

Emily Enki Kim-Vance, this book is for you. Don't you dare become a tattooing pastry chef; go be a physicist. Magne Emo loves you.

My life is perfect, even when it's not. I'm the luckiest girl in the world. Thank you so very much, dear reader, for making it so.

HEATHER KIM is a pastry chef, painter, and a tattoo artist at Minneapolis Tattoo Shop, an all-female owned and operated parlor. Her deliciously unconventional desserts have been praised by the *Minneapolis Star Tribune*, *Minnesota Monthly*, and *Eater*. She lives in Minneapolis, Minnesota, with the loves of her life — her college sweetheart, Scottie, and their schnauzers, Max & Nietzsche.

NOTES

CREDITS

Edited by Donald Lemke   *Ball Buster (cake balls, of course)*

Designed by Bob Lentz   *(. . . and taste-tester)*

Photographed by Karon Dubke   *Feast your eyes, literally*

Recipes baked and styled by Sarah Schuette   *Dessert Diva*

Illustrations by Capstone; **Photographs by** Capstone Studio: Karon Dubke, except: Heather Kim, 80r; Shutterstock: Alexandra Budzinskaya, 131m, Andrei Zveaghintev, 158bl, ang intaravichian, 130l, Becky Starsmore, 130m, George3973, 159tl, igor kisselev, cover (cherry pie), JIANG HONGYAN, 131l, Lotus Images, 158tm, mayakova, 159tm, Nick Lundgren, 29, Olga Popova, 131r, Roman Rybaleov, 158br, sarawutnirothon, 158tr, Sergio33, 159bl, Slavoljub Pantelic, 130r, Tim UR, 158tl, Valentina Razumova, 159r

Artistic elements by Capstone and Shutterstock: bigacis, Duplass, Imageman, kwanchai, Prostock-studio, Saranya Loisamutr, sasimoto, Savvapanf Photo, Valerii__Dex

INDEX